MW00632687

MODERN
Jewish Comfort Food

Modern Jewish Comfort Food

100 FRESH RECIPES FOR CLASSIC DISHES FROM KUGEL TO KREPLACH

Shannon Sarna

Phototography by Doug Schneider

Styling by Sheri Silver

Countryman Press

An Imprint of W. W. Norton & Company
Independent Publishers Since 1923

Printed in the United States of America

For information about permission to reproduce selections from this book, write to
Permissions, Countryman Press, 500 Fifth Avenue, New York, NY 10110

For information about special discounts for bulk purchases, please contact
W. W. Norton Special Sales at specialsales@wwnorton.com or 800-233-4830

Manufacturing by Versa Press
Book design by Laura Palese
Production manager: Devon Zahn

Countryman Press
www.countrymanpress.com

An imprint of W. W. Norton & Company, Inc.
500 Fifth Avenue, New York, NY 10110
www.wwnorton.com

978-1-68268-698-0

10 9 8 7 6 5 4 3 2 1

To Bubbe Phoebe

Contents

Introduction

Comfort food is completely subjective; it varies person to person, family to family, and region to region, even among Jewish families.

For me, the ultimate comfort food is a steaming bowl of egg noodles, lightly buttered with a big dollop of cottage cheese on top and tons of black pepper. It's what my father used to feed me for lunch on Sundays, because it's what his grandfather used to feed him. It's also my mother-in-law's favorite comfort food, one that her own grandmother fed her, and now it is my daughters' favorite, too. For many, this combination may seem bizarre, but for families with Polish heritage, the dish is likely familiar. It's peasant food: simple, cheap, and completely satisfying. It's the dinner we throw together when there's nothing else in the fridge. It's beloved not only because it's delicious but because of the story it tells. In Poland, it contained homemade egg noodles and pot cheese. In America, it received an easier upgrade with store-bought noodles and the more widely available cottage cheese. Some families make it sweet with a little sugar and cinnamon; others, like mine, keep it savory, but it is a common taste of home for families whose great-grandparents, or great-great-grandparents, came over from Poland.

This is merely one vignette of comfort food from American-Jewish-Polish families. What is so enthralling about Jewish comfort food is that it's not a monolith. For Jews from around the world and diverse backgrounds, it means many things and tastes vastly different, but has a few common threads that tie it together: it tells the story of where we have been, our struggles as a people, and how we have persevered.

To say this more simply, the story of Jewish food goes something like this: We were poor, we didn't have a lot, so we threw what scraps we had together and the result was delicious. And by the way, this isn't just the story of how Jewish comfort foods came into existence. This is a theme that runs throughout comfort foods from around the world. As I discovered while growing up half Italian American and half Jewish American, the commonalities between Jewish food stories and Italian food stories (as well as among other cuisines) tell many similar tales of creating deliciousness from very little.

The Jewish people have lived in or been exiled to wide-ranging lands all over the world, which tells a diverse story of our people and foods that have been adopted and adapted by them. Joan Nathan has explained that there isn't so much "Jewish food," as a way of Jewish cooking that has adapted to kosher dietary laws and local cuisines wherever Jews have settled, which is why it's so difficult to succinctly explain what exactly "Jewish food" looks and tastes like: it is so very many things.

Let's take a few minutes to review some Jewish history, and how it has shaped Jewish cuisine.

There are four categories of Jewish people whose lands and histories deeply impact their customs and foods: Ashkenazim, hailing primarily from eastern Europe, Germany, and northern France; Sephardim, Jews of Iberia who were part of the Spanish diaspora (i.e., kicked out during the Spanish Inquisition, which has included Greece, Italy, the Balkans, North Africa, Turkey, and many countries in South America and the Caribbean); Mizrahim, who hail from Middle Eastern countries and who often lived side by side Muslim and Christian neighbors for thousands of years; and Ethiopian Jews, who had been almost completely isolated from other Jewish communities until the 1980s, and so have very special, unique customs.

The majority of American Jews hail from Europe, and with such large waves of Jewish immigrants from Hungary, Germany, Poland, Ukraine, Lithuania, and Russia at the end of the 19th and beginning of the 20th centuries, a brand-new Jewish cuisine emerged from Manhattan's Lower East Side, and other immigrant enclaves around the United States. Deli culture, bagels and lox, and sugar-laden noodle kugels made a deep impact on the ways Jews would cook in America, and also how non-Jewish Americans would define Jewish food. The stereotypes of matzah ball soup, knishes, and brisket, however, doesn't tell the entire story of Jewish American immigration, and leaves out later waves of immigrant communities from Syria, Iran, Greece, and other parts of the Middle East.

The creation of the state of Israel in 1948, and the waves of immigrants who made it their new home, deeply influenced the next chapter of Jewish food. Immigrants from Europe but also many Middle Eastern and North African countries brought their own comfort foods with them, which became part of an evolving new cuisine: flaky Yemenite breads, such as *malawach*, *kubaneh*, *jachnun*, and their rich complementary soups; Iraqi meat-filled *kubeh* dumplings and the traditional eggplant, potato, and egg breakfast that became the popular *sabich* sandwich; thinly pounded, German-style schnitzel; and Palestinian chopped salads and creamy hummus converged and evolved into a new and very dynamic cuisine.

Due to the nature of our global economy today and social media, that new Israeli cuisine has been catapulted around the world, embraced by home cooks and chefs, Jewish and non-Jewish, Israeli and non-Israeli alike. It has changed the way Jews everywhere eat and think about food. We now see that Jewish food can be stuffed cabbage *and* stuffed zucchini, schmaltz *and* tamarind, brisket *and* schnitzel, street knishes *and* homemade *sambousek*. Jewish comfort food encompasses so many things.

Comfort food may mean something different to every community, but it is, ultimately, the smells, sounds, and memories of being in the kitchen. For my Syrian Jewish friends, it's spinach *jibn* for a weekday breakfast, leek patties freshly fried for Rosh Hashanah, and kibbeh on Shabbat. For my Israeli Jewish friends, it means chocolate hazelnut swirl cookies with afternoon tea, shakshuka on busy weeknights, and stuffed peppers for Shabbat dinner. For my own American Jewish family, it is a big slice of noodle kugel at Yom Kippur break-fast, chicken soup with matzah balls and lots of dill on Passover, and sweet-and-sour meatballs just because.

Chef and TV host Pati Jinich once told me that if a cuisine doesn't evolve, it dies. Jewish food continues to shift, expand, and reinvent itself—and it's thrilling to live in a time where people are excited to eat, enjoy, and talk about it. As editor of *The Nosher* for the past 10 years, it has been my daily goal to tell the story of the Jewish people through food and I take this responsibility seriously in that job, and in presenting this book.

One of the pieces of feedback I hear again and again about my book *Modern Jewish Baker* is that the clear instructions, visuals, and recipes give people confidence to tackle baking projects they've never tried before. This served as inspiration for *Modern Jewish Comfort Food*: to provide that same instruction, visual guidance, and accessible recipes to inspire home cooks to tackle new Jewish comfort foods that might previously have felt too daunting. This book showcases a variety of foods, but there are so many more that are not included. I do not claim in any way that this is a comprehensive list, but I hope it will serve to inspire you to explore and keep cooking.

CHAPTER 1

Chicken Soup

Let's talk about making soup.

Well, first let's clarify that there is a difference between chicken soup and chicken stock. Chicken, vegetable, or beef stock is the foundation for any good soup. Stock is not quite the finished product but the base for any great, comforting soup.

Chicken soup has become synonymous with American Jewish comfort food, even referred to as Jewish penicillin. The truth is that Jews don't have a monopoly on chicken soup and the dish truly transcends cultures and traditions. Soups exist in every culture and in every region: from Filipino *caldo* to Japanese ramen, all rely on chicken or bone broths as the foundation for these iconic bowls of warmth and deliciousness.

Ashkenazi Jewish soup is unique in the aromatics used to season the broth, and of course what is put into the soup for serving. Eastern European chicken soup uses root vegetables, chicken bones or parts, parsley or dill (or both), sometimes ginger, and salt and pepper. Yemenite chicken soup gets flavored with a spice blend known as hawaij, adding cumin, coriander, and cardamom for a delicious and warm punch of spice; Greek chicken soup, which predates even Ashkenazi chicken soup, adds lemon and egg to create a creamy, luscious texture. And even within each of these traditions, the exact amounts and spices will vary from family to family and region to region.

Here are a few tips for making chicken soup:

- You must use meat on the bone to make a proper stock. No, you cannot use chicken breasts. Whole chickens, thighs, necks, drumsticks, and even chicken feet are the preferred parts to use. Fat is flavor and essential to making a good stock.
- Always simmer, never boil. You want to draw out the flavors slowly, which means you don't want the soup pot boiling. It should always stay simmering.
- Aromatics are essential, no matter which ones you use. There are lots of different spices, herbs, and vegetables you can add. But they are crucial for helping build up the flavor profile of your soup. I list the ones I like, but you could also add fresh ginger, leeks, fennel, parsley root, sweet potato, cilantro, etc.
- Taste your soup at various stages, and season at those stages as well. If it turns out your soup is too salty, try adding a peeled, raw potato to the soup.
- Soup freezes well and will last for around three months in the freezer. Make sure it cools completely before putting into a container.

Chicken Stock

Makes 6 quarts

The smell of my own grandmother's chicken soup is singed into my nose's memory. I could walk into her house and immediately know whether she had been simmering a pot of soup on the stove. Her chicken soup was distinctive in those little pools of fat shimmering at the top. There wasn't a Jewish holiday at her home in Yonkers, New York, that didn't include that golden broth and little matzah balls.

My own method for making chicken soup does stray from how my grandmother made it, which also differs from how my mother-in-law makes hers, and both are delicious. Every home cook or chef will tell you they recommend a different cut of chicken or combination of cuts for a rich chicken stock. But the most important takeaway is to make sure you are using pieces of chicken that still have some fat and skin on them, for flavor. Bones are key. Chicken feet are great and very traditional, although more challenging to find. My go-to is to use one whole chicken plus wings, but you can use any combination, so learn what you like best or just rely on using what is available to you. When I want to make an extra-rich broth, I add one or two marrow bones and simmer along with the other bones.

1 bunch of parsley
1 bunch of dill
1 tablespoon black peppercorns
1 whole chicken, plus 1 pound chicken wings, chicken drumsticks, thighs, or feet
2 marrow bones (optional)
4 carrots, rough chopped
4 celery stalks, rough chopped
1 large onion, cut in half with skin left on
2 parsnips, rough chopped
1 turnip, cut into quarters
1 teaspoon ground turmeric (optional)
2 to 3 tablespoons kosher salt

1 Make a bouquet garni by placing the parsley, dill, and peppercorns in cheesecloth and tying it closed with kitchen twine. See the Cook's Tip about using a soup sock as an alternative.

2 Place all the remaining ingredients in a large stockpot and cover completely with cold water.

3 Cover and bring to a simmer over medium-high heat.

4 When the soup has started to simmer, remove the cover. As foam begins to gather at the top, skim it off the soup. You will do this for about the first hour of cooking.

5 After about 1 hour of cooking, remove the whole chicken and any chicken parts with meat. Remove the meat from the bones and add the bones back to the pot.

6 Allow the chicken meat to cool. I typically place it in a container in the fridge at this point to use later in the soup or to make into chicken salad.

7 At this point, add a few tablespoons of kosher salt. Continue to simmer the stock, ideally for 5 to 6 hours, but for at least 2 to 3 hours. Remove from the heat, allow to cool, and then strain through a fine-mesh sieve.

8 Store the chicken stock in deli containers in the fridge for 5 days, or in the freezer for 3 months.

COOK'S TIP

There is another easy way of adding your soup ingredients and then straining them, which is a product called a soup sock. It is a mesh bag made from cotton and widely available at home goods stores and online. You can place all your aromatics, and even the chicken pieces, inside this large bag while the soup is simmering.

After the stock has simmered for a few hours, just pull out the sock, making the job of straining a bit easier. Continue to simmer your stock to intensify the flavor.

CLASSIC Jewish Chicken Soup

Serves 4 to 6

After you have made that perfect base stock, here's how to put it all together for some classic, Ashkenazi Jewish American soup. At many Jewish delis in the United States, you can order something called the "mish mosh" soup, which roughly translates to "a little bit of everything," and that's how I love serving chicken soup as well: with a little bit of everything—matzah balls, kreplach, lots of shredded chicken, fresh dill, matzah balls, noodles, and kreplach, if I am really ambitious.

But chicken soup simply on its own is delicious, comforting, and healing. In fact, chicken soup, and other soups made with simmered animal bones, is scientifically proven to help if you have a cold. Those Jewish moms and grandmothers were really on to something.

2 tablespoons olive oil
3 quarts Chicken Stock (page 14)
3 carrots, peeled and sliced
3 celery stalks, sliced
Fresh dill
Salt and freshly ground black pepper
Noodles, matzah balls, or kreplach for serving

1 Heat the olive oil in a large pot over medium heat. Add the carrots and celery and cook for 4 to 5 minutes, until softened slightly.

2 Add the stock to the pot and bring to a boil. Lower the heat to a simmer, add some fresh dill to the pot, and cook for 20 minutes.

3 Season with salt and pepper.

4 Ladle the chicken soup into bowls. Add cooked noodles, rice, boiled kreplach, prepared matzah balls, or all of the above into each bowl of soup. Top with additional fresh dill, if desired.

Note: **If you are serving to kids, it's also super fun to serve with alphabet letter noodles or other fun shapes, such as dinosaurs or Stars of David.**

Homemade Matzah Balls with Dill

Makes 16 to 20 matzah balls

There's no shame in buying a box of matzah ball mix, which already includes matzah meal, seasoning, and baking soda, and just following the directions. In fact, I have interviewed many chefs who swear this is how they make matzah balls. But of course, there are others who swear by actual, homemade matzah balls. The combination of seltzer water and baking powder will help add a lightness to your matzah balls. No matter how you roll them, matzah balls are one of the ultimate comfort foods.

4 large eggs, at room temperature
¼ cup vegetable oil or chicken fat
2 tablespoons seltzer water
1 cup matzah meal
¼ teaspoon baking powder
½ teaspoon salt
1 tablespoon chopped fresh dill
Cooking spray for plate

1 Whisk together the eggs, vegetable oil, and seltzer in a medium bowl. In a separate bowl, combine the matzah meal, baking powder, and salt.

2 Add the matzah meal mixture to the egg mixture, plus the dill, and gently mix with a fork until just combined, taking care not to overmix. Place in the fridge for chill for 30 to 60 minutes.

3 Bring a large pot of water to a boil.

4 Keeping a small cup or bowl of cold water next to you, roll the matzah mixture into walnut-size balls, dipping your hands into the cold water before forming each next ball, and place on a plate greased with cooking spray.

5 Add the matzah balls to the boiling water, cover tightly, and lower the heat to medium. Cook for 30 minutes.

6 Serve with chicken soup.

Vegetarian Stock

Serves 4 to 6

There are lots of times when you may need a good vegetarian stock to use for cooking or to make a meat-free version of chicken soup that is just as rich and flavorful as soup made with bones. You can experiment and try a combination of other vegetables that you may have around or enjoy.

1 large onion, cut in half, skin left on
3 carrots, rough chopped
1 parsnip, rough chopped
3 celery stalks, rough chopped
1 cup button mushrooms, washed
1 cup cherry tomatoes, or 2 plum tomatoes
1 bunch of parsley
A few thyme sprigs
1 tablespoon black peppercorns
1 bay leaf
1 teaspoon ground turmeric
½ cup dried porcini mushrooms
1 cup hot water
Salt and freshly ground black pepper

1 Place the onion, carrots, parsnip, celery, button mushrooms, and tomatoes in a large stockpot or slow cooker.

2 Make a bouquet garni with the parsley, thyme, peppercorns, and bay leaf. Add the bouquet garni to the pot. Add the teaspoon of turmeric on top.

3 Fill the pot with cold water.

4 Bring to a simmer if using a stockpot, or if using a slow cooker, and set it to cook on LOW for 3 to 4 hours.

5 At the end of cooking, cover the dried porcinis with the cup of hot water in a heatproof bowl and steep for 20 minutes. Add the porcini liquid to the pot.

6 Season with salt and pepper to taste.

7 Can be frozen and stored for 2 to 3 months.

Get Scrappy: Save Your Veggie Scraps and Make Soup

This is the kind of "recipe" that isn't really a recipe at all. You can make vegetable stock using just your leftover veggie scraps. Save your carrot peels, celery ends, root vegetable peels, mushroom stems, onion peels, slightly wilted herbs, pepper pieces, zucchini ends, and so on, and store them in a resealable plastic bag in the fridge for a week, or the freezer for 1 to 2 months until you have gathered a full bag of scraps.

Place them in a stockpot with some peppercorns, more herbs, maybe an onion, some cherry tomatoes that have seen better days, or whatever else you have on hand. Fill the pot with water and simmer away. After a few hours, strain off the vegetables and you will have a beautiful vegetable stock that you can use in a variety of recipes.

Yemenite Chicken Soup

Serves 4 to 6

Yemenite Jewish cuisine is not fancy; it is simple, rustic, and epitomizes comfort food. Yemenite cuisine is known for its rich soups, delicate flaky breads, spicy hot sauce called *zhug*, and *hilbeh*, a traditional sauce made from fenugreek. This cuisine was born out of necessity: Yemenites had very little, being very poor in their homeland, but were known to "make magic" with the few ingredients they had. There weren't large quantities of meat at their disposal, which is why they historically had to turn to soups to take some bones, some vegetables and some spices, and to transform it into something so much more—a theme that runs throughout Jewish cuisines from around the world.

Oxtail soup is one of the classic Yemenite soups that people love. The broth is rich and flavorful, and with potatoes and carrots, it's hearty but also simple and comforting. This version is my slightly Americanized version made with marrow bones and hawaij, a traditional Yemenite spice blend that comes in two forms: a savory version for soups and another for coffee, the latter of which has been likened to a Yemenite chai mix.

Yemenite foods have gained some popularity in the United States. You can buy spicy zhug hot sauce at Trader Joe's, and kosher markets often sell frozen versions of Yemenite jachnun, a rolled flaky pastry traditionally served on Shabbat morning, and malawach, a flaky flatbread.

2 tablespoons olive oil
3 carrots, peeled and sliced
3 celery stalks, sliced
1 teaspoon ginger paste or finely minced fresh ginger
2 garlic cloves, minced
3 quarts Chicken Stock (page 14)
2 or 3 marrow bones
2 tablespoons hawaij spice blend (see Note)
1 pound Yukon Gold or fingerling potatoes, sliced
Fresh cilantro (optional)

1 Heat the olive oil in a large soup pot over medium-high heat. Add the carrots and sauté for 4 to 5 minutes, until slightly softened. Add the ginger and garlic and cook for another 2 minutes.

2 Add the stock and bring to a simmer. Add the marrow bones, hawaij spice blend, and potatoes and simmer for around 1 hour, or until the potatoes are tender.

3 Serve the soup with fresh cilantro, the whole marrow bones, and crusty bread so you can spread the marrow on top.

Note: **It's simple enough to make your own spice blend, but you can also buy hawaij at specialty spice shops or a Brooklyn-based company called NY Shuk.**

Savory Hawaij Spice Blend

To make your own savory hawaij for use in soup, combine 1 tablespoon of ground turmeric, 1 tablespoon of ground cardamom, 1 tablespoon of ground coriander, and 1 tablespoon of freshly ground black pepper. Can be stored in an airtight container for 3 months.

Greek Lemon and Orzo Soup

(Avgolemono)

Serves 4 to 6

This creamy, lemony soup is a classic Sephardi dish often served for Yom Kippur break-fast by Jews of Greek, Italian, or Balkan descent. But you can also find this soup on many Greek restaurant menus throughout the United States. Its creaminess actually comes from tempered eggs, which are added to the stock slowly, similar to how you temper eggs when making a custard. It is not a complicated soup to make, and you will find the taste to be both light and soothing.

2 tablespoons olive oil
1 large onion, diced
5 cups Chicken Stock (page 14)
1 cup water
½ cup dried orzo pasta
3 large eggs
Juice of 1 lemon (about ¼ cup)
1½ cups cooked shredded chicken breast
Salt and freshly ground black pepper
Fresh parsley or dill (optional)

1 Heat 2 tablespoons of olive oil in a medium pot over medium heat. Sauté the onion until translucent, 7 to 10 minutes.

2 Add the chicken stock and water and bring to a low boil. Lower the heat to medium and simmer for 10 minutes.

3 Add the orzo, cover, and cook the pasta for 8 to 10 minutes. Add salt and pepper to taste. After the orzo has finished cooking, remove the soup from the heat.

4 Whisk together the eggs and lemon juice in a heatproof glass or nonreactive metal bowl. Slowly ladle 1 cup of the hot soup into the egg mixture, making sure to keep whisking the entire time. Add the tempered eggs and stock back to the pot and turn heat back on at medium-low. Add the shredded chicken to the soup and heat until heated through. **Note:** Do not bring the soup to a boil, or it could curdle the eggs.

5 Serve with fresh parsley or dill, if desired.

Mustard and Dill Chicken Salad

Serves 4

When you simmer an entire chicken in your soup, there will typically be some meat left over. Using up your leftovers and every part of the animal is a deeply ingrained Jewish concept, and I could never just let some good chicken go to waste. My favorite thing to do with that leftover meat is to whip up a quick batch of chicken salad, especially with some of the fresh dill that was also used in the stock. You can serve it with fresh challah rolls (page 75), crackers, or my favorite: on toasted multigrain bread with a few layers of iceberg lettuce.

Leftover soup chicken (about 2 cups)
2 celery stalks, finely diced
¾ cup mayonnaise, or more to preference
3 tablespoons spicy brown or Dijon mustard
1 tablespoon freshly squeezed lemon juice
2 tablespoons chopped fresh dill
½ teaspoon fine sea salt
¼ teaspoon freshly ground black pepper

1 Dice or shred the chicken into bite-size pieces.

2 Combine the mayonnaise, mustard, lemon juice, dill, salt, and pepper in a large bowl.

3 Add the chicken and celery to the mayonnaise mixture and mix until thoroughly combined. Adjust the seasoning to taste.

Italian Lentils and Pasta

Serves 4 to 6

So much Jewish food has roots in the simplest peasant food, and the same can be said for Italian food. My own heritage is Jewish on my dad's side, and Italian on my mother's, so lentils with pasta, or *lenticche e pasta*, is the kind of comfort food that speaks straight to my soul and connects to both traditions. You can make this soup either with the Vegetarian Stock (page 21) or Chicken Stock (page 14). It's great with lots of fresh Parmesan sprinkled on top and some crusty bread for dipping.

1 cup dried green lentils
2 tablespoons olive oil
1 onion, diced
2 carrots, finely diced
1 celery stalk, finely diced
2 garlic cloves, minced
1 tablespoon tomato paste
1 dried bay leaf
⅓ cup dried pasta (smaller is ideal for this; e.g., small shells, elbows, ditalini, or tubettini)
3 cups water
3 cups chicken or vegetable stock
Salt and freshly ground black pepper
Grated Parmesan for serving (optional)

1 Rinse the lentils, removing any broken pieces.

2 Heat the olive oil in a small pot. Add the onion and cook until translucent, 5 to 7 minutes. Add the carrots and celery and cook for another 2 minutes. Then, add the garlic and tomato paste and cook for 1 to 2 additional minutes. Add the rinsed lentils.

3 Add the water and stock and bring to a boil. Lower the heat and simmer for 25 to 30 minutes. Add more liquid if it is cooking too quickly.

4 Add salt and pepper to taste. Serve with grated Parmesan, if desired.

Kosher Ramen-Style Soup

Serves 4 to 6

Of course, ramen is not a dish with Jewish origins, but Chinese and Japanese. But like so many Jewish dishes, ramen started as a "poor man's dish" that was cheap and filling. American Jews have a long-standing relationship with Asian food, especially Chinese food, as Jewish and Chinese immigrants lived side by side in Manhattan's Lower East Side neighborhoods, influencing each other's culture in America. Ramen is also notoriously not kosher, as pork and shellfish often play critical roles in seasoning the stock. I wanted to re-create something similar to ramen but using only kosher ingredients, including homemade chicken stock, since flavorful broth is the foundation for a good, steaming bowl of ramen. My children absolutely love this dish and gobble it up whenever I make it.

2 tablespoons vegetable oil or other neutral oil
2 teaspoons minced fresh ginger or ginger paste
2 garlic cloves, minced
1 tablespoon miso paste
2 quarts Chicken Stock (page 14)
Cooked ramen-style noodles
Asian-Style Braised Flanken (page 30; optional)
Scallions (optional)
Soft-boiled eggs (optional)
Shredded cabbage, julienned carrots, corn, or sautéed spinach or mushrooms (optional)

1 Heat the oil in a large soup pot over medium heat. Sauté the garlic and ginger for 2 to 3 minutes. Add the miso paste and chicken stock and bring to a simmer. Simmer for 20 to 30 minutes.

2 Cook the noodles in boiling water as directed on the package, around 3 minutes. Drain and set aside until ready to serve.

3 After soup has cooked for 20 to 30 minutes, spoon a few ladlefuls of soup into each bowl. Top with the cooked noodles. Other toppings for ramen can include the Asian-Style Braised Flanken, chopped scallions, soft-boiled eggs, shredded cabbage, carrots, corn, or sautéed spinach or mushrooms.

How To Make Soft-Boiled Eggs

The first tip I find helpful about any kind of boiled eggs is to use eggs that may have been sitting in your fridge for a bit; don't use those fresh eggs you just picked up at the farmers' market, as the older eggs will actually peel easier.

Bring water to a boil in a medium saucepan. Make sure there is enough water to fully cover the eggs. Using a spider or slotted spoon, gently place the eggs in the water. Cover tightly, turn off heat, and set a timer for 9 minutes. While the eggs cook, prepare a medium bowl of ice water.

After the 9 minutes, drain the hot water and place the eggs in the ice water. Allow to sit for 10 minutes. Gently tap the eggs on the counter and peel off the shells. Serve right away or store in the fridge for 2 days.

Asian-Style Braised Flanken

Serves 4

Most traditional ramen recipes call for different cuts of pork, which add fat and flavor to the broth, and I wanted to find an equally rich way to include some other luscious meat as part of a kosher-style ramen. We serve this sweet-and-savory braised flanken on top of homemade stock and tons of slurpy ramen noodles.

This flanken recipe could also stand on its own, but if you are serving a crowd, you may want to double it, or try using short ribs. You can make this in a Dutch oven or even a slow cooker. It freezes well after it is cooked.

- 2 or 3 large pieces of bone-in, flat flanken (2 to 3 pounds)
- 1 to 2 cups chicken or beef stock
- ½ cup low-sodium soy sauce
- ⅓ cup light brown sugar
- 1 teaspoon sesame oil
- 1 small knob fresh ginger, peeled
- 2 garlic cloves, peeled and left whole
- ¾ teaspoon Chinese five-spice powder (optional)
- ¼ teaspoon red pepper flakes

1 Preheat the oven to 275°F.

2 Place the meat and remaining ingredients in a large Dutch oven or large casserole dish with a lid. Cover and place in the oven.

3 Check after 1 hour and add more water or stock if the liquid seems to be reducing too much.

4 Cook for 3 to 4 hours in total, until the meat is completely tender. Remove the bones before serving.

Note: **Flanken is popular in a lot of Jewish cooking because it is kosher and has traditionally been considered a less desirable cut, and is therefore cheaper. Flanken is the same cut of meat as short ribs, which typically have a lot of fat and need to be cooked low and slow. Depending on where you live, it may be harder or easier to find Jewish-style flanken. A kosher butcher will know which cut you are looking for. If you are going to a nonkosher butcher, you should ask for the meat to be cut long, flat, and still on the bone. If you cannot get this cut of flanken, short ribs can be used interchangeably.**

CHAPTER 2

Stuffed Vegetables

Let's talk about stuffed vegetables.

There are many variations of stuffed vegetables, and so many cultures from around the world have their own version. Stuffed vegetables originated as a way to take a little bit of meat and to make it stretch much further. Meat was a luxury for Jews, whether it was in Ukraine or Syria, and so taking just a small amount of ground meat, mixing it with rice and vegetables, and then simmering it in flavorful sauces created rich, delicious, and filling fare. These are not the most beautiful dishes, but they are some of the most quintessential homey, comfort foods of the Jewish people.

Today in Israel, stuffed vegetables, or *memulaim* (Hebrew for "stuffed ones"), are a particularly popular dish, which is certainly an influence of both the diversity of Sephardi and Middle Eastern Jews who migrated to Israel, and also the vegetable-forward environment of the country. Israeli cuisine is known for its vibrantly colored salads in part because it has a strong agriculture, and in part because Israelis truly love their vegetables for health-focused reasons. Israel has the largest number of vegans in the world, with around 5 percent of the population saying they are vegan. Vegetarianism and veganism have been growing trends in Israel for many years, and vegetarian versions of traditional dishes are very common.

As a rule, stuffed vegetables are a little bit of what Ashkenazi Jews would call a *patchke*, a Yiddish word meaning that they can be a bit of work. There are multiple steps to create the stuffing, prepare the vegetables, and also make a sauce. This is why they are traditionally served for Shabbat or holidays, and not necessarily as an everyday dish. In this chapter, I am sharing a selection of Jewish stuffed vegetable recipes from diverse traditions, but there are so many more to explore as well.

A few notes about rice: The Syrian stuffed vegetable recipes in this chapter call for basmati rice that is soaked and then gets cooked in the dish. The stuffed cabbage rolls and stuffed peppers call for long-grain white rice that is precooked. In these latter recipes, you can also use raw rice that is soaked and then drained, but I have always had better luck using precooked rice for them. You can substitute basmati or brown rice in any of the recipes.

Here are a few tips to keep in mind for all stuffed vegetables:

- Don't overstuff any of these vegetables. It can be easy to want to shove that stuffing in, but less is more.
- Don't compact the filling—you want to keep it loose so the stuffing (especially those with rice) have room to expand when cooking.
- Make sure the filling and sauce are both seasoned well.
- Stuffed vegetables, such as cabbage and onions, do freeze well and can be reheated.
- Experiment with the fillings and sauces in these recipes—you could absolutely try using the eastern European sweet-and-sour sauce from the cabbage rolls with the stuffed peppers, or the simple vegetarian rice mixture from the stuffed peppers in the cabbage rolls.

Eastern European Stuffed Cabbage

Serves 6 to 8

Stuffed cabbage is a classic eastern European dish of rice and ground beef rolled up in cabbage leaves and simmered in a tomato-based sauce. It is often made for Sukkot and Simchat Torah, when it is traditional to eat stuffed foods. It is also said that the rolls resemble Torah scrolls, a nod to the holiday of Simchat Torah, which celebrates the cycle of reading the Torah in its entirety.

I grew up with stuffed cabbage on my grandmother's holiday table. It was my dad's and uncle's favorite, but as kids, we absolutely never touched it. My grandmother made hers with maple syrup and citric acid, which my grandfather kept around because he was a food chemist. My husband's grandmother, Baba Billie, made hers with raisins and lemon juice; and now when my father makes it at home, he uses a jar of sauerkraut. I've seen recipes that use grape jelly, or even cocktail sauce.

The bottom line is that this sauce can be made in a variety of ways. The essential elements are to include tomatoes, something sweet, and something for acidity.

1 large green or savoy cabbage (see Note on page 37)

For the filling:

1 pound ground beef
¼ cup cooked long-grain white rice (or whatever cooked rice you have around)
1 small onion, grated (around ½ cup)
1 large egg
1 teaspoon salt
½ teaspoon freshly ground black pepper
¼ cup unseasoned bread crumbs

For the sauce:

2 tablespoons olive oil
1 small onion, diced
½ apple, peeled, cored, and grated
One 15-ounce can tomato sauce
1½ cups stock (chicken or vegetable is fine)
¼ cup white or apple cider vinegar
2 tablespoons light brown sugar
¼ cup raisins
½ teaspoon ground cinnamon
½ teaspoon salt
¼ teaspoon freshly ground black pepper

1 **Prep the cabbage:** Bring a large pot of water to a boil. Using a paring knife, remove the core from the cabbage. Dunk the cabbage into the boiling water. After 2 to 3 minutes, the leaves will start to soften and you can remove the layers. Repeat until you have around 16 leaves.

2 **Make the filling:** Place the ground beef, cooked rice, onion, egg, salt, and pepper in a medium bowl and combine. Add the bread crumbs and mix in evenly. Set aside.

3 **Make the sauce:** Heat the olive oil in a saucepan over medium heat. Sauté the onion and apple for 5 to 7 minutes, until the water has cooked out and the onion is softened and starts to become golden. Add the tomato sauce, stock, vinegar, brown sugar, raisins, cinnamon, salt, and pepper. Bring to a simmer over medium-low heat and cook for 5 minutes.

4 Cover the bottom of an 8-by-13-inch Pyrex baking dish with a thin layer of sauce, about one-quarter of the sauce.

5 Remove the tough stem in the middle of the cabbage leaves, using a paring knife.

recipe continues

6 Scoop the rice mixture into an approximately ½-cup oval (smaller leaves might require less filling). Place the scoop of filling in the middle of a cabbage leaf and fold in the sides. Roll up the cabbage leaf and place, seam side down, in the prepared baking dish. Repeat with the remaining cabbage leaves and filling. You may have some cabbage left over. You can discard it, add it to soup, or chop it up and add it to the sauce, if desired.

7 Add the remaining sauce over the top. Cover with foil and bake for 1½ hours, or until the color of the cabbage has changed from bright green to a duller green, the sauce has reduced slightly, and the cabbage rolls can easily be cut into.

Note: **You can use any leafy green you like; it actually doesn't have to be cabbage. Green cabbage is probably the most traditional to use, although I do find it can be harder to make the rolls using a standard green cabbage. Savoy cabbage leaves are sturdier and make the rolling easier, but they don't end up yielding quite the same tender result.**

Vegetarian Stuffed Cabbage Rolls

Serves 6 to 8

Israelis have been well ahead of the curve with promoting plant-based, vegan foods, and have found many ways to re-create meat-free versions of family-favorite recipes. This vegetarian version of stuffed cabbage uses finely chopped mushrooms instead of meat to combine with rice as the filling. You could also use a plant-based meat alternative, if you prefer. If you want to make this dish vegan, you can just leave out the egg in the filling and add a little bit of water or stock to moisten the mixture and to ensure it holds together.

If you want a milder filling, you could also use the simple rice filling from the Vegetarian Israeli Stuffed Peppers (page 47).

1 head green or savory cabbage

For the sauce:

1 small onion, diced

½ apple, peeled, cored, and grated

One 15-ounce can tomato sauce

1½ cups stock (chicken or vegetable is fine)

¼ cup white or apple cider vinegar

2 tablespoons light brown sugar

¼ cup raisins

½ teaspoon ground cinnamon

½ teaspoon salt

¼ teaspoon freshly ground black pepper

For the filling:

2 tablespoons olive oil

1 tablespoon unsalted butter (optional)

1 large onion, diced

12 to 14 ounces button or baby bella mushrooms, cleaned and diced

2 garlic cloves, minced

1 tablespoon soy sauce

1 tablespoon tomato paste

2 teaspoons fresh thyme leaves

1 teaspoon dried oregano

15 ounces (½ cup) dried porcini mushrooms

1½ cups cooked long-grain white or brown rice

1 large egg

1 teaspoon fine sea salt

½ teaspoon freshly ground black pepper

1 **Prep the cabbage:** Bring a large pot of water to a boil. Using a paring knife, remove the core from the cabbage. Dunk the cabbage into the boiling water. After 2 to 3 minutes, the leaves will start to soften and you can remove the layers. Repeat until you have 16 leaves.

2 **Make the sauce:** Heat the olive oil in a saucepan over medium heat. Sauté the onion and apple for 5 to 7 minutes, until the water has cooked out and the onion is softened and starts to become golden. Add the tomato sauce, stock, vinegar, brown sugar, raisins, cinnamon, salt, and pepper. Bring to a simmer over medium-low heat and cook for 5 minutes.

3 **Make the filling:** Heat the olive oil and butter (if using) in a large sauté pan. Cook the onion and mushrooms until completely soft, around 10 minutes. Add the garlic and cook for another 2 minutes. Add the soy sauce, tomato paste, thyme, and oregano and cook for another 1 to 2 minutes. Remove from the heat and allow to cool.

4 While the mushrooms are cooking, pour 1 cup of hot water over the dried porcini mushrooms and allow to sit for 20 minutes. After 20 minutes, remove and chop the mushrooms. Combine the button mushroom mixture, rice, egg, porcini mushrooms, salt, and pepper in a medium bowl.

5 Remove the tough stem in the middle of the cabbage leaves using a paring knife. Cover the bottom of an 8-by-13-inch Pyrex baking dish with a thin layer of the sauce, about one-quarter of the sauce.

6 Scoop the rice mixture into an approximately ½-cup oval (smaller leaves might require less filling). Place the scoop of filling in the middle of a cabbage leaf and fold in the sides. Roll up the cabbage leaf and place, seam side down, in the prepared baking dish. Repeat with the remaining cabbage leaves and filling.

7 Add the remaining sauce over the top. Cover with foil and bake for 1½ hours, until the color of the cabbage has changed, the sauce has reduced slightly, and the cabbage rolls can easily be cut into.

Stuffed Eggplant

Serves 4

Israelis love eggplant, but more broadly, Jews have a long-standing history and love affair with the vegetable. Eggplants actually originated in India and were brought to Spain, where they became a dietary staple. When Jews were kicked out during the Spanish Inquisition, they carried eggplants with them to diverse lands. But eggplants also thrive in the Mediterranean climate, and so eggplants easily thrive in Israel, where they grow all year and are not expensive. Eggplants are truly revered in Israel, where you can find them roasted, baked, cooked, and mixed in innumerable forms.

This dish is a slightly simpler recipe than some of the other stuffed vegetables in this chapter, since the eggplant doesn't require a ton of hollowing out or complicated preparation. The combination of eggplant and ground meat is hearty and rich.

1 large or 2 smaller eggplants
4 to 5 tablespoons olive oil
Salt and freshly ground black pepper
1 pound ground beef or lamb
2 teaspoons paprika
1 teaspoon ground cinnamon
1 teaspoon ground cumin
1 teaspoon ground coriander
¾ teaspoon fine sea salt
1½ cups water or Chicken Stock (page 14)
3 tablespoons tomato paste
Juice of ½ lemon
Easy Tahini Sauce (page 86) for serving (optional)
Fresh herbs for serving (optional)

Notes: **Instead of the beef or lamb, you can use ground turkey.**

Eggplant and tahini are a common combination since their flavors complement each other so well. I suggest serving this dish drizzled with Easy Tahini Sauce (page 86).

1 Preheat the oven to 400°F.

2 Cut the eggplant(s) down the middle. Brush the inside of each with 2 to 3 tablespoons of olive oil and sprinkle with salt and pepper.

3 Place on a baking sheet and roast for 20 minutes. Remove from the oven and allow to cool slightly.

4 Heat the remaining 2 tablespoons of olive oil in a sauté pan. Add the meat to the pan and cook, breaking the meat into small pieces with a wooden spoon. When the meat is cooked, add the paprika, cinnamon, cumin, and coriander to the pan.

5 Combine the water or stock, tomato paste, and lemon juice in a small bowl. Pour the combined mixture into the bottom of a large baking dish.

6 Place each eggplant half, skin side down, in the baking dish. Fill each portion of eggplant equally with the meat filling. Cover the top of the baking dish tightly with foil.

7 Lower the oven temperature to 350°F and bake for 1 hour.

8 To serve, drizzle with the Easy Tahini Sauce and fresh herbs, if desired.

Syrian Stuffed Zucchini

with Tamarind and Apricots

Serves 4 to 6

Mehshi is the Arabic word for these types of stuffed vegetables, and there are many kinds, including stuffed tomatoes, artichokes, baby eggplant, potatoes, onions, and zucchini. The filling, known as *hashu*, is used in a number of dishes. This stuffed zucchini is a classic in almost every Syrian family, and is common throughout the eastern Mediterranean region known as the Levant (Syria, Lebanon, Jordan, Palestine, and Israel). The filling may vary, as does the sauce, but meat and rice stuffed into hollowed-out zucchini is a beautiful and comforting dish. If you end up with extra filling, roll it into meatballs and cook them nestled alongside the zucchini.

For the zucchini:

¾ cup uncooked basmati rice
8 medium to large zucchini (see Notes)
1 pound ground beef
1 teaspoon ground allspice
½ teaspoon ground cinnamon
1 teaspoon salt
½ teaspoon freshly ground black pepper
1 tablespoon olive oil
20 dried apricots

For the sauce:

3 tablespoons tamarind paste (see Notes)
¼ cup sugar
2 cups water or Chicken Stock (page 14)

Notes: **Try to pick out zucchini that are a bit thicker, so it is easier to hollow them out and to stuff them. I would strongly suggest buying a zucchini corer to make this recipe. It's a minimal investment, and it can also be used to core apples.**

Tamarind paste can vary; some is less or more sour. So, make sure to taste your sauce and add more sugar or honey if it is too tart for your taste.

1 Soak the rice in cold water for 30 minutes. Drain.

2 **Make the sauce:** Combine the tamarind paste, sugar, and 2 tablespoons of the water in a small saucepan. Bring to a boil, then allow to reduce for 3 to 5 minutes. Remove from the heat and set aside.

3 Preheat the oven to 325°F.

4 **Make the zucchini:** Combine the ground beef, soaked basmati rice, allspice, cinnamon, salt, pepper, and the olive oil in a bowl.

5 Using a zucchini corer, hollow out the middle of the zucchini. Cut each zucchini in about three lengths of equal size.

6 Gently stuff each piece of zucchini, taking care to not compact the stuffing, and also leaving space for it to expand.

7 Stand the zucchini on end, filling side up, in a large, oven-safe saucepan, pouring the sauce all around the zucchini. Tuck the apricots between the zucchini pieces. If you have additional filling and have turned it into meatballs, place them alongside and in between the zucchini.

8 Bring the sauce to a boil over medium-high heat and then cover.

9 Place the pan in the oven and bake for 40 to 50 minutes, checking halfway through to make sure there is enough liquid.

10 Remove from the oven and allow to rest for 15 to 20 minutes before serving.

Make It Passover-Friendly

To make this dish Passover-friendly, or even just lower-carb, replace the basmati rice with cauliflower rice.

Syrian Stuffed Onions

with Pomegranate Sauce

Serves 4 to 6

There is something just so beautiful about stuffed onions all lined up in a pan, to say nothing of how delicious is the combination of sweet onions, rich meat filling, and tangy pomegranate sauce. Stuffing the onions can be a little tricky. It is very important to buy the large Vidalia or Spanish onions, otherwise if your onions are too small, it will make this task nearly impossible. If you cannot find those, the largest onions you can find are your best choice.

You could use ground lamb, ground turkey, or ground chicken for this recipe. If you swap out the beef for turkey or chicken, add an extra tablespoon of oil and a tablespoon of water to the filling mixture to ensure it stays moist.

⅓ cup uncooked basmati rice

For the onions:

4 large Spanish onions

For the meat filling:

1 pound ground beef
1 onion, very finely grated or diced (½ cup)
2 tablespoons vegetable oil
½ teaspoon ground allspice
½ teaspoon ground cinnamon
¼ teaspoon dried mint (optional)
1 teaspoon kosher salt
½ teaspoon freshly ground black pepper
¼ cup pine nuts (optional)

For the sauce:

1 cup pomegranate juice
1 cup vegetable, chicken, or beef stock, or water
2 tablespoons pomegranate molasses
1 tablespoon honey

For assembly:

2 tablespoons olive oil
2 garlic cloves, minced

1 Soak the rice in cold water. Set aside until ready to prepare the filling, and then drain.

2 **Prepare the onions:** Bring a medium pot of water to a simmer.

3 Peel the outer layer of the onions, while keeping as much of the end intact. Cut a slit vertically down the side of each onion, without cutting all the way through. You will use this later to help peel apart the onion layers from each stuffed onion.

4 Place the onions in the simmering water and allow to cook for 15 to 20 minutes over medium-low heat until soft and the layers are peeling. Remove from the pot and set aside to cool.

5 **Make the meat filling:** While the onions are simmering, combine the ground beef, grated or diced onion, drained rice, vegetable oil, allspice, cinnamon, dried mint (if using), salt, pepper, and pine nuts (if using).

6 **Make the sauce:** Combine the pomegranate juice, stock or water, pomegranate molasses, and honey in a small bowl.

7 Once the onions have cooled and the meat mixture is prepared, begin stuffing each onion. Work carefully to detach each layer by sticking your finger gently under each layer of onion and separating. If the inside layers aren't soft enough, stick them back into the simmering water until they have softened enough to separate. Hold the curved side of the onion cupped in your hand and spoon around 1 tablespoon of filling into each layer of onion.

8 Preheat the oven to 350°F.

9 Heat the olive oil in a Dutch oven, or other large, oven-safe pot, over medium heat. Sauté the garlic for 1 to 2 minutes. Turn off the heat. Place the stuffed onions, seam side down, in the Dutch oven and gently pour the sauce over the onions.

recipe continues

10 Place in the oven and bake for 2 hours.

11 Remove from the oven and allow to rest for 15 to 20 minutes before serving.

Note: **You will not end up using the entire onion that you grate—I typically wrap up the rest of it and use it for another dish I am making.**

Make It Passover-Friendly

To make this dish Passover-friendly, or even just lower-carb, replace the basmati rice with cauliflower rice.

Israeli Stuffed Peppers with Meat

Serves 4

Many Israelis I know have a strong connection to stuffed peppers. They make an appearance at least once a week, either served on Shabbat because they were easy to cook and required much less prep work than other stuffed vegetables, or they were served as a weeknight meal, when there might be little bits and bobs of leftover vegetables or meat from the week, which easily transformed into a filling for stuffed peppers.

Israeli-style stuffed peppers are likely inspired by Bulgarian Jewish immigrants, who cooked stuffed peppers in a delicately spiced tomato sauce. Today, stuffed pepper recipes will vary family to family: sometimes the sauce is made with ketchup and water; other times, it combines canned tomatoes, basil, thyme, and oregano. Some are stuffed with ground lamb or chicken and rice, whereas others might be stuffed with just rice, nuts, and spices.

For the filling:

2 tablespoons olive oil

1 small or ½ large onion, diced

1 cup cooked basmati or other long-grain white rice

8 ounces ground beef

¼ cup pine nuts

1 tomato, grated (best to hand grate on a coarse grater)

¾ teaspoon paprika

1 tablespoon chopped fresh parsley, or ½ teaspoon dried

¼ teaspoon salt

⅛ teaspoon freshly ground black pepper

For the sauce:

One 15-ounce can tomato sauce

½ cup water

3 garlic cloves, minced

1 tablespoon honey

¼ teaspoon salt

5 to 6 bell peppers, seeds and inner membranes removed (you can leave top of peppers intact for presentation, if desired)

1 Preheat the oven to 350°F.

2 **Make the filling:** Heat the oil in a large sauté pan over medium heat. Sauté the onion until translucent. Add the meat and break up with the back of a wooden spoon. Cook until the meat is no longer pink, around 5 minutes.

3 Mix together the rice, ground beef, pine nuts, grated tomato, paprika, parsley, salt, and black pepper in a bowl. Add the sautéed onion and combine.

4 **Make the sauce:** In a separate bowl, combine all the sauce ingredients.

5 Scoop the filling into each bell pepper until filled three-quarters of the way. Place the "lid" of each pepper on top (this step is optional). Take care not to overstuff each pepper.

6 Place the stuffed peppers in a large baking dish. Pour the sauce all around the peppers. Cover the baking dish tightly with foil and bake for 50 to 60 minutes, until peppers are soft.

7 Serve warm.

Note: **To prepare a bell pepper, start by slicing a small piece off the bottom of the pepper so that it stands upright in the pan. Slice a piece off the top, about ½ inch thick, to form the lid of the pepper. Using a small paring knife, remove and discard the white pith and seeds inside the pepper.**

Make It in a Slow Cooker

To make this recipe in a slow cooker, spray the inside of a slow cooker with cooking spray. After step 4, place the stuffed peppers in the slow cooker and pour the sauce over them. Cook on HIGH for 3 to 4 hours, or on LOW for 7 to 8 hours.

Vegetarian Israeli Stuffed Peppers

Serves 4

Stuffed peppers are a staple in Israeli homes, and offer endless variation. My friend Ruth calls hers "garbage peppers," because she uses up all the odds and ends from her fridge to stuff into peppers. Many Israeli families I know make their own versions and serve them every week for Friday night dinner. These stuffed peppers are perfect as a side dish, or as a vegetarian main that can be adjusted according to taste and what you have on hand.

For the filling:

1 cup cooked long-grain white rice
1 medium onion, grated (⅓ to ½ cup)
1 tomato, grated
1 tablespoon olive oil
1 teaspoon salt
½ teaspoon freshly ground black pepper
2 tablespoons minced fresh dill
2 tablespoons minced fresh parsley

4 bell peppers (I like using a mix of colors)

For the sauce:

One 15-ounce can tomato sauce
2 cups Vegetarian Stock (page 21) or Chicken Stock (page 14)
2 garlic cloves, minced
2 teaspoons honey
Juice of ½ lemon
½ teaspoon fine sea salt
¼ teaspoon freshly ground black pepper

1 **Prepare the filling:** Combine the rice, onion, tomato, olive oil, salt, black pepper, dill, and parsley in a bowl.

2 **Prepare the peppers:** Start by slicing a small piece off the bottom of the pepper so that it stands upright. Cut off and reserve the very tops of the peppers with their stems. Remove and discard the ribs and seeds from inside the peppers, using a small paring knife.

3 Fill each pepper three-quarters of the way up with the rice filling. Do not pack tightly—the rice will need room to cook and expand.

4 **Make the sauce:** Combine the tomato sauce, stock, garlic, sugar, lemon juice, salt, and black pepper in a large saucepan.

5 Place the filled peppers in the pot of sauce. Top each pepper with its reserved top and stem.

6 Cook, covered, over low heat for about 1 hour, or until the peppers are completely tender and the rice is fully cooked. Season the sauce to taste with additional salt and black pepper.

Make It Cheesy!

You could add some crumbled or grated cheese to the rice mixture, prior to stuffing, if you want to make this dish a bit cheesy.

- *Variation 1: Add 4 ounces of crumbled feta to the rice mixture.*
- *Variation 2: Add ½ cup of corn kernels and 1 cup of shredded Cheddar to the rice mixture. Add extra shredded Cheddar on top once stuffed into the peppers.*

CHAPTER

3

Kugel

Let's talk about kugel.

Kugel is considered a nearly sacred food by many Ashkenazi Jews, but it is a term that encompasses many types of dishes. And by the way, kugel is almost exclusively an Ashkenazi dish.

Kugel is a Yiddish word, originating from High German, which literally means "sphere," a reference to the way it puffed up when it was baked. Kugel in its very first iterations was more of a bread dumpling, morphing first into noodle kugel and then later to potato kugel as potatoes were introduced in eastern European diets sometime around the mid-18th century.

There are two main varieties of kugel—potato and noodle—but kugels can and are made with a variety of ingredients today: noodles, potato, vegetables, and even matzah. The basic elements for any kugel are some kind of starch, fat, and eggs. Kugel can be served warm or at room temperature, which is why it is most often served on Shabbat or Jewish holidays, when fire is not used. Having dishes that can be warmed or at a low temperature was traditionally important, and is relevant still today for those who observe the laws of Shabbat. Kugel is also most often served with a meat meal, which means dairy cannot be included in the kugel if they are to be served together, and so most kugels you will encounter are pareve (containing neither meat nor dairy). The exception is dairy noodle kugel, which originated in Europe and transformed in America.

Kugel has evolved over time, and can vary greatly depending on the region where it originates. For example, noodle kugels from Poland and Hungary tend to be sweeter, where it was easier to grow cane, than those from Lithuania or Russia, where kugels lean more on the savory side. Some noodle kugels incorporate fruit, whereas others are simpler. Upon arriving in America, like so many things, noodle kugels became sweeter and transformed into truly American creations but remain a highly beloved comfort food.

Here are some tips for making kugel:

- Size matters. That is, the size of your pan will make a difference in the consistency of your kugel. You will notice some recipes call for a 9-by-11-inch pan; others call for 9-by-13-inch. You can use either, but some recipes do come out better with a thicker kugel, and others with a bigger pan that yields a thinner kugel. Of course, use what you have, but the recommended size is intentional.
- If you like an extra-crispy kugel, pour a few tablespoons of olive oil into your pan and place the pan in the preheated oven while preparing the rest of the dish. When the kugel batter is ready, remove the heated pan and add the batter to the sizzling oil. This will help ensure a crispy crust all the way around.
- Make sure to grease your pan well, and also allow the kugels to cool slightly before slicing into them, as they may fall apart more if they are still too hot.
- Most kugels can be made ahead of time and reheat well, making them ideal dishes to serve on holidays and Shabbat.
- Most kugels freeze well. You should make sure to let them cool completely and then freeze them in pieces, wrapped in parchment paper or foil, and then placed in a resealable plastic freezer bag.

Salt and Pepper Noodle Kugel

Serves 8 to 10

Most North American Jews are familiar with sweet noodle kugels. But there are also many savory noodle kugel varieties, which can include garlic, onions, mushrooms, or even spinach. This kugel is a recipe from my husband's grandmother, Baba Billie. It has an extra garlic kick, fantastic mouthfeel, and a nice crunchy top. You can use fresh garlic if you want, but I think the jarred garlic in oil really is the preferred ingredient.

One 12-ounce package wide or extra-wide egg noodles
3 to 4 heaping tablespoons olive oil
6 large eggs
2 tablespoons jarred garlic in oil, or minced fresh garlic
1 tablespoon garlic powder
1½ teaspoons fine sea salt
1 teaspoon freshly ground black pepper
Paprika
Coarse sea salt (optional)

1 Preheat the oven to 375°F. While the oven is heating, pour the olive oil into a 9-by-13-inch glass baking dish and place the dish in the oven for the oil to heat. This step will make for a crispier kugel.

2 Boil the noodles in a large pot of salted water according to the package directions, around 5 minutes. Drain and set aside.

3 While the noodles are cooking, whisk together the eggs, garlic, garlic powder, fine sea salt, and pepper.

4 Add the drained noodles to the egg mixture and mix gently until completely coated. Remove the baking dish from the oven and add the noodles. They will sizzle slightly—this is exactly what you want. Spread out the noodles evenly in the dish.

5 Sprinkle the top with paprika and coarse sea salt, if using. Bake, uncovered, for 40 minutes, or until the noodles achieve your desired crispiness.

6 Serve warm or at room temperature.

Gina's Hungarian Noodle Kugel

Serves 8 to 10

Several years ago, my dear friend Merisa Fink invited me to have Shabbat dinner with her family. Her mother, an amazing cook, served this Hungarian noodle kugel, her own mother's recipe that is handwritten and framed in her kitchen. I fell in love and asked my friend's mom, Gina, to teach me to make it. Noodle kugels vary from family to family and region to region, and this noodle kugel was unlike anything I had ever tasted. Like kugels originating in Poland, Hungarian noodle kugel also leans on the sweet side.

Unlike most of the other kugel recipes I am sharing that mix in the eggs all at the same time, this kugel mixes the egg yolks into the noodle filling itself, and uses the egg whites as a topping along with ground nuts, sugar, and lemon zest. The result is a fluffy noodle base with a sweet and slightly crunchy topping.

For the filling:

Cooking spray for baking dish
1 pound fine egg noodles
10 large egg yolks
⅓ cup sugar
½ cup + 1 tablespoon vegetable oil or melted margarine

For the topping:

10 large egg whites
8 ounces ground walnuts or almonds
½ cup + 2 tablespoons sugar
½ cup golden raisins
Zest of 2 lemons

1 **Make the filling:** Preheat the oven to 325°F. Grease a 9-by-11-inch baking dish with cooking spray.

2 Boil the noodles in a large pot of salted water according to the package directions, 3 to 5 minutes.

3 Drain the noodles, coat with the tablespoon of vegetable oil, and allow to cool.

4 Mix together the egg yolks and sugar in a medium bowl.

5 In a separate bowl, combine the drained noodles with the remaining ⅓ cup of vegetable oil.

6 **Make the topping:** Beat the egg whites in a large bowl until stiff. Fold in the ground nuts, raisins, and lemon zest in two or three batches until combined, taking care not to remove too much air from the egg whites.

7 Pour the noodles into the prepared baking dish. Spoon the topping on top, swooping with the back of the spoon to make little mounds.

8 Bake, uncovered, for 35 to 40 minutes, until the topping is golden brown.

9 Remove from the oven and allow to cool slightly before cutting into pieces.

Sweet Dairy Noodle Kugel

Serves 8 to 10

If you asked your average American Jew about noodle kugel, the answer would probably most closely resemble this recipe with butter, cottage cheese, and some kind of sweet, crunchy topping. In truth, this type of sweet kugel was a later addition for European Jews and most likely had farmer cheese (sometimes referred to as pot cheese) as the dairy component, whereas most other kugels are pareve (nondairy) so that they can be enjoyed on Shabbat or holidays when meat is most likely consumed. At the time that kugel arrived on American shores, the sweet noodle version was most prevalent, largely due to the origins of those immigrants.

During the 20th century, Jews made all kinds of changes to kugel based on what was in fashion, and many of those changes persist today. Raisins were replaced with canned pineapple or fruit cocktail. Cornflake topping was also a midcentury addition, reflecting how American Jewry adopted broader culture into their own practices and traditions.

Personally, I never tasted a noodle kugel with dairy until I was a teenager, as we grew up with one sweet and savory noodle kugel, or lokshen pudding as my grandmother called it, for holidays (*lokshen* is the Yiddish word for "noodles"). But the minute I tasted this variety of sweet cheese-infused kugel I understood why American Jews embraced it so fully. It is decadent and almost dessertlike.

This kugel recipe lends itself to endless variations: swap out the raisins for dried cranberries or dried cherries. You could also use crushed pineapple or fruit cocktail. In addition to the kugel base itself, you can also play around with your toppings, although you can leave your kugel naked on top. Many Ashkenazi American Jews make a sweet dairy noodle kugel like this for Yom Kippur break-fast or Shavuot, when it is traditional to eat dairy foods. It is also great for brunch, or as a nurturing dish to bring someone in need of a comforting meal, like a new mom.

This recipe is inspired by my dear friends Yuval and Sarah Brokman, who make this kugel for every special occasion, but you can make it anytime you need a batch of comfort food.

For the base kugel:

Cooking spray for baking dish

1 pound wide egg noodles

8 tablespoons (1 stick) unsalted butter, at room temperature

2 cups granulated sugar

8 ounces full-fat cream cheese, at room temperature

6 large eggs, beaten

2 teaspoons vanilla extract

2 cups full-fat or 4% cottage cheese

¼ cup raisins (optional)

1 **Make the base kugel:** Preheat the oven to 400°F. Grease a 9-by-11-inch baking dish with cooking spray.

2 Boil the noodles in a large pot of salted water according to the package directions, around 5 minutes.

3 While the noodles are cooking, using a handheld mixer and a large bowl or a stand mixer fitted with the whisk attachment, beat the butter and granulated sugar for 2 minutes. Add the cream cheese and continue to mix until smooth, another 1 to 2 minutes. Add the eggs, vanilla, cottage cheese, and raisins, if using, and combine.

4 When the noodles are cooked, drain thoroughly and stir into the egg mixture by hand.

5 **Make the topping:** Combine the melted butter, cornflake crumbs, brown sugar, and salt in a bowl.

6 Pour the kugel mixture into the prepared baking dish. Sprinkle the cornflake mixture evenly over the top of the kugel.

For the topping:

8 tablespoons (1 stick) unsalted butter, melted

¾ cup cornflake crumbs

½ cup packed light brown sugar

¼ teaspoon fine sea salt

7 Bake, uncovered, for 40 to 45 minutes.

8 Remove from the oven and allow to cool slightly before cutting. Serve warm or at room temperature.

Topping Variations

GRAHAM CRACKERS

¾ cup graham cracker crumbs

½ cup light brown sugar

¼ teaspoon fine sea salt

6 tablespoons unsalted butter, melted

SALTINES

¾ cup saltine crumbs

½ cup light brown sugar

6 tablespoons unsalted butter, melted

BISCOFF COOKIES

½ cup Biscoff cookie crumbs

¼ cup graham cracker crumbs

¼ cup light brown sugar

¼ teaspoon fine sea salt

6 tablespoons unsalted butter, melted

Pineapple Upside-Down Kugel

Serves 6 to 8

Pineapple was one of the fruits added to sweet noodle kugels in the mid-20th century in America as it became a fashionable fruit. Since sweet kugel can often feel a bit like dessert instead of a side dish, I decided to have a little fun with this recipe and combine classic pineapple upside-down cake with a traditional noodle kugel, using sour cream, crushed pineapple, and of course that caramelized pineapple and maraschino topping. You will want to take out your nicest cake stand to present this whimsical mash-up.

Cooking spray for pan

For the topping:

4 tablespoons (½ stick) unsalted butter, melted

¾ cup packed light brown sugar

8 or 9 canned pineapple rings, drained of excess liquid

8 or 9 maraschino cherries

For the base kugel:

8 tablespoons (1 stick) unsalted butter, at room temperature

4 large eggs

½ cup granulated sugar

1 teaspoon vanilla extract

One 12-ounce package wide egg noodles

8 ounces full-fat sour cream

10 ounces canned, crushed pineapple, drained

¼ teaspoon salt

Special equipment:

9- or 10-inch springform pan

1 Preheat the oven to 350°F. Grease a 9- or 10-inch springform pan with cooking spray. Line the bottom of the springform pan with parchment paper.

2 **Make the topping:** Combine the melted butter with the brown sugar in a medium bowl. Spread on the bottom of the prepared springform pan.

3 Arrange one pineapple slice in the center of the pan and the remaining slices around it. Place a cherry in the center of each pineapple slice. Set aside.

4 **Make the base kugel:** Place the butter in a large bowl. In a separate bowl, whisk together the eggs, granulated sugar, and vanilla.

5 Boil the noodles in a large pot of salted water according to the package directions, around 5 minutes.

6 Drain the noodles and pour into the bowl that contains the butter.

7 Add the egg mixture to the noodles and combine. Add the sour cream, crushed pineapple, and salt and mix again.

8 Pour the noodle mixture on top of the fruit in the springform pan.

9 Bake for 40 to 45 minutes. Remove from the oven and allow to cool for 20 minutes before removing from the pan.

10 Run an offset or silicone spatula around the sides of the kugel to separate it from the pan. Place a serving platter or large plate on top of the kugel and turn upright quickly so the pineapple and cherries are on top.

11 Serve warm or at room temperature.

Yerushalmi Kugel

Serves 4 to 6

Yerushalmi, or Jerusalem, kugel is truly a unique and delicious dish. This kugel is a marriage between Europe and the Middle East that tells its own story of the Jewish people's migration. Eastern European Jews brought the concept of kugel (what is really a word of German origin) to Jerusalem in the 18th and 19th centuries. Traditional noodle kugel transformed slightly, influenced by Sephardi flavors, with lots of black pepper and sugar to caramelize slowly as it bakes. It's peppery, sweet, and very special.

One of my culinary idols, Israeli cookbook author and food editor Janna Gur, combines wide and thin egg noodles in her Yerushalmi kugel and I have always loved the contrasting texture of both sizes and also the beautiful way it looks. This recipe uses thin noodles, but you can do it half and half, 6 ounces each of wide egg noodles and thin egg noodles; just take care to cook them separately, as they cook for different lengths of time.

Cooking spray for pan
12 ounces thin egg noodles
⅓ cup + 1 tablespoon neutral oil, such as vegetable, canola, or sunflower
4 large eggs
2 teaspoons fine sea salt
2 teaspoons freshly ground black pepper
1 teaspoon ground cinnamon
1 cup sugar
Coarse sea salt (optional)

1 Preheat the oven to 325°F. Grease a 10-by-5-by-3-inch loaf pan with cooking spray and set aside.

2 Boil the noodles in a large pot of salted water according to the package directions, around 5 minutes.

3 Drain the noodles. Coat the cooked noodles with the tablespoon of oil and set aside.

4 Beat the eggs in a bowl with the fine sea salt, pepper, and cinnamon, then set aside.

5 Heat the remaining ⅓ cup of oil and the sugar in a medium saucepan over medium heat, stirring constantly, for around 5 minutes, or until it becomes golden brown. The oil will separate slightly and that's normal. You don't want the caramel to burn.

6 When the caramel is done, immediately pour on top of the noodles, stirring to coat. Some of the sugar will harden; this is also normal. Add the egg mixture slowly, mixing it in completely.

7 Pour into the prepared pan.

8 Top the kugel batter with coarse sea salt, if desired. Cover with foil and bake for 1½ hours.

9 Remove from the oven and allow to cool slightly before slicing.

Mac & Cheese Kugel

Serves 6 to 8

Is it just mac & cheese? Is it a kugel? It doesn't really matter because this American-comfort-food-meets-Ashkenazi casserole will be an instant hit for brunches, Yom Kippur break-fast, or dinner anytime you need to feed a crowd.

For the base kugel:

Cooking spray for dish

18 ounces wide egg noodles

6 large eggs

8 ounces mild Cheddar, shredded

4 ounces Velveeta or American cheese, cubed, shredded, or cut into small pieces

4 tablespoons (½ stick) unsalted butter

1 cup sour cream

For the topping:

1 cup buttery crackers, such as Ritz

8 tablespoons (1 stick) unsalted butter, melted

2 tablespoons grated Parmesan

1 **Make the base kugel:** Preheat the oven to 350°F. Spray a 9-by-13-inch baking dish with cooking spray.

2 Boil the noodles in a large pot of salted water according to the package directions, around 5 minutes. Drain the noodles.

3 While the noodles are cooking, place the eggs, Cheddar, Velveeta, butter, and sour cream in a large bowl and mix. Add the hot, drained noodles to the bowl and mix until everything is combined.

4 Pour the noodles into the prepared baking dish.

5 **Make the topping:** Combine the cracker crumbs, melted butter, and Parmesan in a small bowl.

6 Sprinkle the top of the kugel evenly with the cracker mixture.

7 Bake for 35 to 40 minutes, until golden on top.

8 Remove from the oven and allow to cool slightly before cutting into squares for serving.

Potato Kugel

Serves 8 to 10

Potato kugel came into existence several hundred years after noodle kugel, as potatoes were introduced in Europe and eastern Europe in the mid-1700s and early 1800s, respectively, eventually becoming a staple of the Ashkenazi Jewish diet. Cheese latkes were replaced by potato latkes, and Ashkenazi Jews love to joke about their poor digestive tract related to all the potatoes they ate in Russia. All joking aside, potato kugel is just as delicious as noodle kugel with its crispy edges and creamy interior, and serves as a perfect accompaniment to a hearty braised meat dish, or alongside roast chicken, too.

My husband's grandmother, Baba Billie, was the kugel master in the Goldberg family. My husband has now taken on the title, having learned how to make almost all Baba Billie's kugels at her side. It's not a holiday in our house without Jonathan's potato kugel. One of the secrets to this kugel is heating the oil in the baking dish so that when you pour the potato mixture in, it will sizzle. This allows the outside to become crispy all over.

⅓ cup olive oil
8 medium Yukon Gold potatoes, peeled
2 medium-large onions
5 large eggs
¾ cup matzah meal or gluten-free matzah meal
1½ tablespoons fine sea salt
2 teaspoons freshly ground black pepper
2 teaspoons garlic powder
Sweet or hot paprika
Coarse sea salt

1 Preheat the oven to 375°F. While the oven is heating, pour the olive oil into a 9-by-13-inch glass or Pyrex baking dish and place the dish in the oven for the oil to heat up.

2 Whisk the eggs together in a large bowl.

3 Using a food processor or the coarse side of a hand grater, shred the potatoes and onion together into a large bowl.

4 Add the shredded potato and onion, matzah meal, fine sea salt, pepper, and garlic powder to the bowl. Mix until combined.

5 When the oil has heated for about 10 minutes, remove the baking dish from the oven.

6 Add a small spoonful of the potato mixture, and if it starts sizzling, it is hot enough. If not, put the baking dish back into the oven for a few minutes.

7 When the oil is ready, add the entire potato mixture and spread in an even layer, using an offset spatula or large spoon.

8 Sprinkle the top with paprika and coarse sea salt.

9 Bake for 40 to 50 minutes, until crispy around the edges and golden brown on top.

10 Remove from the oven and allow to cool slightly before cutting into squares.

11 Serve warm or at room temperature.

recipe continues

Note: **This kugel uses matzah meal as a binder, which means it can also be made for Passover, when conventional wheat-based products (such as noodles or bread crumbs) are not consumed.**

Triple Veggie Kugel

Serves 6 to 8

This is a variation on potato kugel that also incorporates zucchini and carrots. Zucchini have a lot of water, so make sure to wring out as much liquid as possible before adding to the potato mixture. My friend Rachel Ringler makes a similar version using a few tablespoons of fresh dill, which I think adds a really nice note of fresh herbs, though you can leave out the dill if you prefer.

⅓ cup olive oil
1 large zucchini (around 1 pound)
4 Yukon Gold potatoes (around 1½ pounds)
4 medium carrots (around 1 pound)
1 onion
4 large eggs
¾ cup matzah meal or bread crumbs, or gluten-free matzah meal
1 tablespoon fine sea salt
1 teaspoon onion salt
2 teaspoons freshly ground black pepper
Coarse sea salt (optional)

1 Preheat the oven to 375°F.

2 While the oven is preheating, pour the olive oil into a 9-by-13-inch glass or Pyrex baking dish and place the dish in the oven for the oil to heat up.

3 Whisk the eggs together in a large bowl.

4 Using a food processor or the coarse side of a hand grater, shred the zucchini. Place in a tea towel and remove the excess liquid. Separately grate the potatoes, carrots, and onion.

5 Add the eggs, shredded vegetables, matzah meal, fine sea salt, onion salt, and pepper. Mix until combined.

6 When the oil has heated for about 10 minutes, remove the baking dish from the oven.

7 Add a small spoonful of the vegetable mixture, and if it starts sizzling, it is hot enough. If not, put the baking dish back into the oven for a few minutes.

8 When the oil is ready, add the kugel mixture and spread in an even layer, using an offset spatula or large spoon.

9 Sprinkle the top with coarse sea salt, if desired.

10 Bake for 55 to 60 minutes, until crispy around the edges and golden brown on top.

11 Remove from the oven and allow to cool slightly before cutting into squares.

12 Serve warm or at room temperature.

Jojo's Cakey Crunch Sweet Potato Kugel

Serves 6 to 8

Inspired by a Jewish vegetable kugel and an American dump cake, this Thanksgiving kugel is a unique expression of how American Jews have so fully embraced American traditions. My mother-in-law, Jodi (aka Jojo to all the grandchildren), started making this sweet potato kugel for Thanksgiving about 10 years ago, and from the moment we all tasted it, we fell in love. It's easy to make and a true crowd-pleaser.

- **8 medium sweet potatoes, peeled and cut into quarters**
- **1 tablespoon vanilla extract**
- **3 tablespoons light brown sugar**
- **½ teaspoon pumpkin pie spice**
- **½ teaspoon kosher salt**
- **¼ cup orange juice or orange-flavored liqueur**
- **Cooking spray for baking dish**
- **8 ounces mini marshmallows**
- **One 15.25-ounce box yellow cake mix**
- **16 tablespoons (2 sticks) unsalted butter or nondairy margarine, melted**

1 Boil the sweet potatoes in a large pot of water until tender, 20 to 25 minutes.

2 Preheat the oven to 350°F.

3 Drain the sweet potatoes and mash in a large bowl. Add the vanilla, brown sugar, pumpkin pie spice, salt, and orange juice and mix well.

4 Grease a 9-by-11-inch baking dish with cooking spray. Evenly spread half of the sweet potato mixture in the prepared baking dish.

5 Sprinkle the marshmallows evenly over the top. Add the remaining sweet potato mixture on top of the marshmallows and spread evenly, using an offset spatula or knife.

6 Sprinkle the yellow cake mix (dry, straight from the package) evenly over the top of the sweet potato mixture. Pour the melted butter or margarine evenly over the cake mix.

7 Bake for 60 minutes, or until slightly browned on top. Serve warm or at room temperature.

CHAPTER 4

Shakshuka

Let's talk about shakshuka.

Shakshuka is a North African dish made from tomatoes, hot pepper or hot sauce, and eggs. Brought to Israel by Libyan and other North African Jewish immigrants, the exact origin is unknown but shakshuka has become one of the most popular dishes of Israel and has also exploded onto brunch menus at restaurants literally all over the world. *Shakshuka* means "all mixed up" in Arabic, and indeed it is a dish that can be quite mixed up because it can be made nearly 1,000 different ways, depending on the cook, season, or ingredients on hand.

Although the most classic shakshuka is made primarily with tomatoes, since tomatoes grow well in the Mediterranean region, many other types of "shakshuka" have since developed, including sauces made without tomatoes at all. The dish has become so popular and mainstream that you can buy shakshuka starter kits in many major supermarket chains. Trader Joe's even sells a frozen shakshuka starter, and with a little extra seasoning, it's not half bad in a pinch.

Israeli cookbook author and editor Janna Gur calls shakshuka "forgiving and versatile," and that truly explains some of why this dish is so beloved: anyone can make it with very few ingredients. There's not a whole lot that is complicated about making shakshuka. It can be made with ingredients that are local and fresh, or that are all found in your pantry. It's great for a special brunch on the weekends, but it's also perfect for a weeknight dinner when all you've got is some canned tomatoes and eggs hanging around the house.

Here are some tips for making and storing shakshuka:

- You can use fresh or pantry ingredients.
- Cook your sauce for at least 15 to 20 minutes.
- Add your eggs just at the end, and watch them carefully to ensure they don't overcook.
- Shakshuka sauce (without the eggs) can be stored in the fridge for up to 1 week, or frozen for 1 to 2 months.

What Goes with Shakshuka? Everything!

One of the fun parts about making shakshuka is adding your own ingredients and making it a full, healthful meal. Here are just a few ideas of other ingredients to add to your shakshuka sauce. You can do this for just the last few minutes of cooking.

- Sautéed mushrooms
- Roasted eggplant
- Spinach, baby kale, or other greens
- Crumbled feta or goat cheese
- Mini mozzarella balls
- Seared tofu
- Chickpeas
- Sausage
- Lamb Meatballs (page 111)

Basic Tomato and Pepper Shakshuka

Serves 2 to 4

Tomato and pepper shakshuka is the most traditional version of shakshuka and also happens to be my favorite. Although it's not a dish I grew up eating with my own family, I fell deeply in love with it during numerous trips I took to Israel. Although you could serve pita bread or any crusty bread with shakshuka for sopping up all that perfect sauce, I actually prefer to serve mini challah loaves (page 75) alongside shakshuka, not only because it is delicious, but I always thought it was something just a little extra special.

2 to 3 tablespoons olive oil
1 large onion, finely chopped
1 jalapeño or other hot pepper, seeded and finely diced
1 roasted red pepper, chopped
3 garlic cloves, minced
1 tablespoon tomato paste
2 to 3 tablespoons harissa paste (optional)
1 tablespoon paprika
1 teaspoon ground cumin
¼ teaspoon caraway seeds
One 28-ounce can diced tomatoes
1 teaspoon salt
½ teaspoon freshly ground black pepper
½ to 1 cup water or vegetable stock (optional)
3 or 4 large eggs
Fresh parsley, mint, and/or cilantro (optional)

1 Heat the oil in a large sauté pan over medium heat.

2 Add the onion and cook until translucent, 5 to 7 minutes. Add the jalapeño, garlic, and roasted red pepper and cook for another 2 minutes.

3 Add the tomato paste, harissa, paprika, cumin, and caraway seeds and continue to cook for 3 to 4 minutes, until fragrant.

4 Add the diced tomatoes, salt, and black pepper and simmer over medium heat for 15 to 20 minutes. If you prefer the sauce a little thinner, add ½ to 1 cup of water or vegetable stock.

5 When the sauce has reached your desired consistency, crack each egg, one at a time, into a small glass bowl and then gently add to the tomato sauce. Cover and cook for 3 to 5 minutes, until the whites have set and the yolks are to your liking.

6 Sprinkle with fresh herbs (if using) before serving.

Note: **You can purchase harissa at many supermarkets, in the global foods aisle. I recommend buying Mina or NY Shuk brand harissa, if you can find it.**

How To Roast Peppers

You could just chop up your peppers before adding to shakshuka sauce, but I love the smokiness of roasted peppers. It's easy enough to buy them jarred at a store, but roasting your own is a simple and satisfying task.

I have a gas range and place the peppers right on top of the open flame to roast, turning them several times until they are charred all over. If this makes you nervous or you don't have a gas range, you can also arrange them on a baking sheet and place under the broiler for 3 to 5 minutes on each side.

After the peppers are charred on all sides, remove from the stovetop or oven and place in a plastic or paper bag to rest. When they have cooled, remove the skin and inside membrane. Now the peppers are ready to use.

SERVE WITH

Small-Batch Challah Rolls or Mini Loaves

Makes approximately 8 mini loaves, 12 rolls, or 1 full-size challah loaf

One of my fondest food memories in Israel was enjoying a quiet, solo lunch at a small café in the heart of Tel Aviv. I ordered the shakshuka, and to my surprise, it arrived alongside an individual challah loaf, freshly baked in a cast-iron pan. Since then, I love serving shakshuka with mini challah loaves for dipping into the sauce.

You can bake this challah into any shape you like, including a traditional braided loaf, challah rolls, or mini loaves. I like using 5½-by-3-inch pans for mini loaves.

For the dough:

1½ tablespoons active dry yeast

¾ cup + ½ teaspoon sugar

1¼ cups lukewarm water

5 cups unbleached bread flour

1½ teaspoons fine sea salt

¼ cup vegetable or other neutral oil, plus more for rising

2 large eggs

For the topping:

1 large egg, beaten

Sesame seeds, poppy seeds, nigella seeds, and/or coarse sea salt

1 **Make the dough:** Combine the yeast, ½ teaspoon of sugar, and lukewarm water in a small bowl. Allow to sit for 5 to 10 minutes, until it becomes foamy on top.

2 Mix together 1½ cups of the bread flour, the fine sea salt, and the remaining ¾ cup of sugar in a stand mixer fitted with the whisk attachment. After the yeast mixture has become foamy, add to the flour mixture along with the oil. Mix thoroughly.

3 Switch to the dough hook and add the remaining 3½ cups of bread flour and the eggs. Mix on low speed for 1 minute, then increase the speed to high and mix for 3 to 5 minutes, until the dough is smooth and pulling away from the side of the bowl.

4 Place the dough in an oiled bowl and cover with plastic wrap or a clean, damp towel. Let rise for 2 to 3 hours at room temperature, or overnight in the fridge.

5 Preheat the oven to 350°F. Divide the dough into the number of loaves you will be baking. Braid and place into the loaf pan(s).

6 Allow to rise for another 25 minutes.

7 **Add the topping:** Brush the top of challah dough with the beaten egg and top with seeds or coarse sea salt, if desired.

8 Bake mini loaves for 20 to 22 minutes, bake a single, traditional loaf for 23 to 25 minutes. They are done when golden brown on top and, when you knock on the bottom, the challah sounds hollow.

9 Remove from the oven and allow to cool slightly before serving.

Basic Tomato and Pepper Shakshuka

Mexican-Inspired Shakshuka

Smoky Vegan Shakshuka

Basic Tomato and Pepper Shakshuka with sausage

Smoky Vegan Shakshuka

with Crispy Chickpeas

Serves 2 to 4

Classic tomato shakshuka is already vegetarian-friendly. But if you want a vegan alternative, this flavorful version made with chipotle pepper and crispy, roasted chickpeas will hit the mark.

For the shakshuka sauce:

2 to 3 tablespoons olive oil
1 large onion, finely chopped
3 garlic cloves, minced
1 tablespoon tomato paste
2 teaspoons paprika
1 teaspoon ground cumin
One 28-ounce can diced tomatoes
2 tablespoons chipotles in adobo sauce
1 teaspoon salt
½ teaspoon freshly ground black pepper
½ to 1 cup water or vegetable stock (optional)
3 or 4 large eggs
Fresh parsley, mint, and/or cilantro (optional)

For the crispy chickpeas:

One 15-ounce can chickpeas, drained and rinsed
1 teaspoon paprika
½ teaspoon fine sea salt
½ teaspoon ground coriander
½ teaspoon freshly ground black pepper
1 tablespoon olive oil

1 **Make the sauce:** Heat the oil in a large sauté pan over medium heat.

2 Add the onion and cook until translucent, 5 to 7 minutes. Add the garlic and cook for another 2 minutes.

3 Add the tomato paste, paprika, and cumin and continue to cook for 3 to 4 minutes until fragrant.

4 Add the diced tomatoes, chipotles in adobo, salt, and black pepper and simmer over medium heat for 15 to 20 minutes. If you prefer the sauce a little thinner, add ½ to 1 cup of water or vegetable stock.

5 **Make the crispy chickpeas:** While the suce is cooking, Preheat the oven to 375°F.

6 Place the chickpeas on a baking sheet. Sprinkle with the paprika, sea salt, coriander, black pepper, and olive oil. Toss all together until the chickpeas are evenly coated with seasoning.

7 Roast in the oven for 12 to 15 minutes, until crispy and golden.

8 Sprinkle with fresh herbs, if desired, before serving.

Mexican-Inspired Shakshuka

Serves 2 to 4

Many cuisines from around the world have their own eggs-baked-in-tomato-sauce dish, including the Italian-inspired "eggs in purgatory" and *chilaquiles*, which is slightly different, but also uses a vegetable sauce, tortilla chips, and eggs to create a hearty yet cheap meal.

This Mexican-inspired shakshuka is an American-Mexican-Israeli mash-up, but super fun when you want to change things up and add some avocado and lime on top of your shakshuka. If you really want to get fancy, fry your own tortilla chips, and add some Mexican Cotija on top.

2 to 3 tablespoons olive oil
1 large onion, finely chopped
1 jalapeño or other hot pepper, seeded and finely diced
1 roasted red pepper, chopped
3 garlic cloves, minced
1 tablespoon tomato paste
1 teaspoon ground cumin
1 teaspoon smoked paprika
1 teaspoon dried oregano
1 teaspoon dried coriander
1 teaspoon chili powder
One 28-ounce can diced tomatoes
1 teaspoon salt
½ teaspoon freshly ground black pepper
½ to 1 cup water or vegetable stock (optional)
3 or 4 large eggs

For serving:
Lime wedges
Fresh cilantro
1 ripe avocado, peeled, pitted, and sliced
Restaurant-style tortilla chips
Cotija (optional)

1 Heat the oil in a large sauté pan over medium heat.

2 Add the onion and cook until translucent, 5 to 7 minutes. Add the jalapeño, garlic, and roasted red pepper and cook for another 2 minutes.

3 Add the tomato paste, cumin, smoked paprika, oregano, coriander, and chili powder and continue to cook for 3 to 4 minutes, until fragrant.

4 Add the diced tomatoes, salt, and black pepper and simmer over medium heat for 15 to 20 minutes. If you prefer the sauce a little thick, add ½ to 1 cup of water or vegetable stock.

5 When the sauce has reached your desired consistency, crack each egg into a small glass bowl, one at a time, and then gently add to tomato sauce. Cover and cook for 3 to 5 minutes, until the whites have set and the yolks are to your liking.

6 Serve with lime wedges, fresh cilantro, sliced avocado, tortilla chips, and Cotija, if desired.

Shakshuka Pizza

Serves 2

Shakshuka pizza is my favorite Israeli-Italian-American mash-up. If the combination sounds weird, just think of shakshuka as a spiced tomato sauce, which makes it perfect to spread on top of some store-bought pizza dough. Served as a cheesy deep-dish pizza with runny eggs on top, this dish is comfort food at its best and perfect as a weeknight dinner. If you don't have a cast-iron pan for this, you can also use a square or round cake pan.

All-purpose flour, for dusting
1 pound store-bought pizza dough
Cooking spray or vegetable oil for pan
1 cup shredded mozzarella
1½ to 2 cups prepared tomato shakshuka sauce
2 to 3 large eggs
1 to 2 ounces feta cheese, plus more for topping
Fresh basil or parsley (optional)

Special equipment:
8- or 9-inch cast-iron pan

1 Preheat the oven to 450°F. Place an 8- to 9-inch cast-iron pan in the oven to heat for at least 20 minutes.

2 On a lightly floured surface, spread out the pizza dough until you have created a circle slightly larger than your pan.

3 Using a good-quality oven mitt, remove the hot pan from the oven. Coat the inside of the pan with cooking spray or an even layer of vegetable oil.

4 Carefully place the dough in the pan. Sprinkle the mozzarella on top of the dough. Spread the shakshuka sauce on top, then sprinkle with the feta.

5 Place the pan back in the oven for 7 minutes.

6 Remove from the oven, and with the back of a spoon, create two or three circles for the eggs. Gently crack each egg into a small glass bowl and pour, one at a time, into the indentations.

7 Bake for another 4 to 6 minutes, until the eggs are cooked to your liking.

8 Top with additional feta, and fresh basil or parsley, if desired.

Green Shakshuka

Serves 2 to 4

Greek shakshuka is a newer, more modern interpretation of the traditional tomato and pepper-heavy dish. Israeli chefs started using all kinds of vegetables, adding eggs and calling it shakshuka. I first tasted a white shakshuka made with eggplant and other vegetables at a shakshuka cart in Manhattan nearly 10 years ago. Green versions of shakshuka have cropped up all over the world and are a great way to cook lots of healthy greens. I suggest using spinach and baby kale, but you can use any greens you have on hand or prefer: collard greens, kale, escarole, or Swiss chard are all great options.

One variation is to add a heaping tablespoon of zhug, pesto, or chimichurri to the greens before cooking the eggs to add some extra flavor or heat.

6 to 8 ounces fresh spinach
6 to 8 ounces baby kale
2 tablespoons olive oil
1 large onion, finely diced
2 garlic cloves, minced
1 jalapeño pepper, seeded and finely diced
1 cup vegetable stock or greens' cooking water, plus more if needed
1 teaspoon ground cumin
1 teaspoon fine sea salt
½ teaspoon freshly ground black pepper
3 or 4 large eggs

For serving:
Fresh herbs, such as parsley, mint, or dill
Sumac (optional)
Feta (optional)

1 Bring a large pot of water to a simmer. Blanch half of the greens in the water until they are just wilted, 30 to 60 seconds, and then remove from the pot. Reserve the cooking liquid.

2 Place the blanched greens in a food processor and pulse for 1 minute with ½ cup of the cooking liquid. Set aside, reserving the remaining cooking liquid if using later instead of stock.

3 Heat the olive oil in a large sauté pan. Add the onion and cook until translucent, 5 to 7 minutes. Add the jalapeño and garlic and cook for another 2 minutes.

4 Add the remaining uncooked greens to the sauté pan and cook until wilted.

5 Add the pureed greens and the cup of vegetable broth or reserved cooking liquid from the greens.

6 Season with the cumin, salt, and black pepper and cook for 10 minutes. If you want a little more liquid to your sauce, add additional vegetable stock or reserved cooking water at this point and cook for another 2 minutes.

7 Crack each egg into a small glass bowl, one at a time, and then gently add to the sauce. Cover and cook for 3 to 5 minutes, until the whites have set and the yolks are to your liking.

8 Serve with chopped fresh herbs, sumac, and crumbled feta, if desired.

Summer Tomato Shakshuka

Serves 2 to 4

Tomatoes are in season nearly year-round in Israel, which is one of the reasons shakshuka is such a popular dish throughout the region. But having access to fresh local tomatoes all year may not be the reality for everyone. This shakshuka uses the most of fresh summer tomatoes.

1 large onion, finely chopped
1 jalapeño or other hot pepper, seeded and finely diced
1 roasted red pepper, chopped
3 garlic cloves, minced
1 tablespoon tomato paste
2 to 3 tablespoons harissa paste (optional)
1 tablespoon paprika
1 teaspoon ground cumin
¼ teaspoon caraway seeds
6 large beefsteak (Jersey) tomatoes or 8 plum (Roma) tomatoes (approximately 3 pounds), rough chopped
1 cup cherry tomatoes, sliced in half
½ teaspoon sugar or honey (optional)
1 teaspoon salt
½ teaspoon freshly ground black pepper
½ to 1 cup water or vegetable stock (optional)
3 or 4 large eggs
Fresh parsley, mint, and/or cilantro (optional)

1 Heat the oil in a large sauté pan over medium heat.

2 Add the onion and cook until translucent, 5 to 7 minutes. Add the jalapeño, garlic, and roasted red pepper and cook for another 2 minutes.

3 Add the tomato paste, harissa paste, paprika, cumin, and caraway seeds and continue to cook for 3 to 4 minutes until fragrant.

4 Add the chopped and cherry tomatoes, sugar, salt, and black pepper and simmer over medium heat for 20 to 30 minutes. If you want the sauce a little thinner, add ½ to 1 cup of water or vegetable stock. You can also choose to remove some of the sauce and puree it if you like it less chunky.

5 When the sauce has reached your desired consistency, crack each egg, one at a time, into a small glass bowl, and then gently add to the tomato sauce. Cover and cook for 3 to 5 minutes, until the whites have set and the yolks are to your liking.

6 Sprinkle with fresh herbs, if desired, before serving.

Easy Tahini Sauce

Makes 1 cup

Tahini sauce is a staple ingredient on any Israeli table. Tahini is made from ground-up sesame seeds, and the taste is nutty, rich, and has endless uses. I love serving tahini sauce on top of roasted vegetables, especially cauliflower and carrots. But it's also the perfect accompaniment for shakshuka. Drizzle some right on top, or serve on the side for dipping with bread and the shakshuka sauce.

½ cup good-quality tahini
⅓ cup ice water, or more
Juice of ½ lemon
½ teaspoon salt
¼ teaspoon freshly ground black pepper

1 Place the tahini in a small bowl.

2 Add the ice water slowly and whisk. Keep adding ice water and whisking until a smooth consistency is reached. Don't worry if the tahini seems too thick at first—just keep drizzling in the cold water and it will smooth out.

3 Add the lemon juice, salt, and pepper. Taste and adjust the seasoning.

Quick and Easy Hummus

Makes 2 cups

When in Israel, most certainly the best meal to enjoy is breakfast, when a traditional spread may include salty white cheese, various chopped salads, tahini sauce, shakshuka, and hummus. And so, for me, it's hard to serve shakshuka without also some accompanying salads, tahini sauce, and a bowl of humus.

Americans consider hummus the perfect snack or dip, whereas Israelis are masterful at turning a bowl of hummus into a full meal. You can serve a big platter of this hummus with chicken, lamb, or vegetarian meatballs right on top, bread for dipping, and a simple chopped salad. Of course, you can serve this as a snack all on its own, or alongside shakshuka for a well-rounded brunch.

- One 15-ounce can chickpeas, drained and rinsed
- ¼ cup tahini
- ½ teaspoon ground cumin
- ½ teaspoon salt
- Juice of 1 lemon
- 2 garlic cloves
- ¼ cup olive oil
- ⅓ to ½ cup cold water
- 1 to 2 tablespoons extra-virgin olive oil for serving
- Paprika, sumac, or za'atar for serving (optional)

1 Start by removing the skins from the outside of the chickpeas. This will take a little time and patience, but will yield a smoother result.

2 Place the skinned chickpeas, tahini, cumin, salt, lemon juice, and garlic in a food processor and start pulsing. While the food processor is running, drizzle in the olive oil. Add ⅓ cup of the water. Taste and adjust the seasoning. Add more water if it feels too chunky or thick.

3 Spoon onto a plate and drizzle with the extra-virgin olive oil. Sprinkle with paprika, sumac, or za'atar to taste.

4 Can be made ahead; store in the fridge for up to 1 week.

Note: **It will take a little effort to remove all those chickpea skins, and you can skip this step if you prefer a chunkier hummus.**

CHAPTER
5

Schnitzel

Let's talk about schnitzel.

Schnitzel, in its most basic definition, is a piece of thinly pounded meat that is breaded and then fried. It was brought to Israel by Austrian immigrants in the 1930s. In Austria, it had been made primarily with veal, which was both expensive and harder to come by once in Israel, and so schnitzel started to be made almost exclusively with chicken.

Israelis truly embraced schnitzel and transformed it into something all their own. Schnitzel is an everyday dish, one that has been adapted many times over and is beloved by almost all Israelis. Some families marinate the chicken before breading and frying; some use homemade bread crumbs made from white bread; others use panko bread crumbs; and still others use matzah meal all year-round, not just when it is Passover. In almost all Israeli versions, sesame seeds are added to the bread crumb mixture, and seasoning will vary from just salt and pepper to paprika, turmeric, and other spices.

Schnitzel is a quintessential dish in Israel and can be found everywhere: in home kitchens, in the frozen foods section, or stuffed inside fluffy pita. And you may be surprised to know that some of the best schnitzel you will find in Israel is actually sold at roadside gas station cafés.

Israelis will also "schnitzel" (meaning to bread and fry) almost anything, including fish, veggies, steak, and tofu.

Here are some tips for making and storing schnitzel:

- If you're using chicken, save yourself some time and buy thinly cut chicken cutlets. Or, if you buy your meat directly from a butcher, ask specifically for thin-cut. This will save you prep time.
- Take care not to overcook your schnitzel—whether you are frying chicken or vegetables, these thin cuts will cook quickly. A few minutes on each side until golden brown should do it.
- Add a pinch of salt on top after you have fried it—the salt will cling to the hot oil and enhance the flavor.
- Schnitzel freezes well; let cool completely, then layer the pieces between parchment paper and double wrap in foil before placing in a resealable plastic freezer bag.
- To reheat, unwrap and place frozen schnitzel on a wire rack in a 300°F oven until crispy.

CLASSIC

Chicken Schnitzel

Serves 4 to 6

Every family will have its way to make chicken schnitzel, and this recipe was taught to my husband by his beloved grandma, Baba Billie, of blessed memory. As legend has it, Baba Billie would prepare a heaping pile of crispy fried chicken schnitzel as a mere snack before the full Shabbat dinner, so her grandchildren could all steal pieces off the counter as they waited eagerly for dinner together. Of course, this recipe is sufficient to serve as a very satisfying dinner all on its own. This recipe includes half panko bread crumbs and half traditional unseasoned bread crumbs. The panko adds great crunch, while the traditional bread crumbs will help evenly coat the chicken, though you could opt for one or the other if that's all you have in your pantry.

3 large eggs
1½ tablespoons spicy or yellow mustard
1 tablespoon water
1 cup panko bread crumbs
1 cup unseasoned bread crumbs
1 teaspoon salt, plus more for sprinkling
½ teaspoon freshly ground black pepper
½ teaspoon paprika
1 teaspoon dried parsley
3 tablespoons sesame seeds
2 pounds thinly cut chicken breasts
Vegetable oil for frying

1 Combine the eggs, mustard, and water in a large bowl or shallow baking dish. Combine the panko and unseasoned bread crumbs, salt, pepper, paprika, parsley, and sesame seeds in another large bowl or shallow baking dish.

2 Dredge each chicken cutlet in the egg mixture, then in the bread crumb mixture, pressing down to ensure the entire piece is covered. Lay flat on a plate or baking sheet. Repeat until all the pieces are covered.

3 Pour the oil to 1 to 1½ inches' depth into a large sauté pan over medium-high heat. You can check to see whether the oil is ready to fry by placing a wooden spoon in the oil; if bubbles start to form around the spoon, it is ready to start frying.

4 Fry the chicken cutlets in batches, two or three at a time, until golden on each side. Depending on the thickness of the chicken, this will take around 3 minutes per side. Take care not to overcrowd the pan, or the chicken will not cook properly.

5 Remove the chicken from the pan and transfer to a wire rack.

6 While the chicken is still hot from the pan, sprinkle each cutlet with an additional pinch of salt.

Note: **Bread crumbs may fall off the chicken while frying. You can use a sieve or spoon to remove some from the oil in between frying batches. If the oil gets too dark, pour out and add fresh oil to help prevent the schnitzel from burning.**

recipe continues

SERVE WITH

Honey Mustard Dipping Sauce

Makes about ½ cup

Whenever I make this creamy honey mustard sauce, there's not a drop left to be found. If you like things a little spicy, try adding 1 to 2 heaping tablespoons of prepared horseradish.

⅓ cup spicy brown or yellow mustard
3 tablespoons honey
2 tablespoons mayonnaise
¼ teaspoon freshly ground black pepper

1 Combine all the ingredients in a bowl.

2 Can be stored in the fridge in an airtight container for 1 to 2 weeks.

Coconut-Crusted Schnitzel Fingers

Serves 4 to 6

Coconut-crusted shrimp is a popular dish in America, and is said to have originated somewhere either in Southeast Asia or the Caribbean, where both seafood and coconut are common ingredients. Of course, shrimp is not a kosher ingredient, so creating a fried coconut schnitzel is a way to re-create these flavors for a kosher kitchen. Sweet coconut and crunchy bread crumbs is a delicious combination. If you like a little extra sweetness, go ahead and use sweetened shredded coconut instead of unsweetened.

2 large eggs
1 tablespoon hot sauce
2 tablespoons water
1¼ cups panko bread crumbs
¾ cup shredded unsweetened coconut
1 teaspoon fine sea salt, plus more for sprinkling
½ teaspoon freshly ground black pepper
2 pounds thinly cut chicken breasts

1 Combine the eggs, hot sauce, and water in a large bowl or shallow baking dish. Combine the panko bread crumbs, coconut, salt, and pepper in another large bowl or shallow baking dish.

2 Dredge each chicken cutlet in the egg mixture, then in the bread crumb mixture, pressing down to ensure the entire piece is covered. Lay flat on a plate or baking sheet. Repeat until all the pieces are covered.

3 Pour the oil to 1 to 1½ inches in depth into a large sauté pan over medium-high heat.

4 Fry the chicken cutlets in batches, two or three at a time, until golden on each side. Depending on the thickness of the chicken, this will take around 3 minutes per side. Take care not to overcrowd the pan, or the chicken will not cook properly.

5 Remove the chicken from the pan and transfer to a wire rack.

6 While the chicken is still hot from the pan, sprinkle each cutlet with an additional pinch of sea salt.

SERVE WITH

Sweet & Spicy Sriracha Mayo

Makes 1 cup

¾ cup mayonnaise
2 to 3 tablespoons sriracha sauce
1 tablespoon sweet chili sauce or honey

1 Combine all the ingredients in a small bowl.

2 Can be stored in airtight container in the fridge for 1 to 2 weeks.

Passover-Friendly Schnitzel

Serves 4 to 6

Passover week can be a challenging time for feeding families, when bread products and pasta are off limits. It is easy to make a Passover-friendly schnitzel by basically replacing the bread crumbs with matzah meal. If you prefer not to use matzah meal, you could replace it with potato chips or taro chips pulsed in a food processor.

Salt and freshly ground black pepper
2 large eggs, beaten
2 teaspoons kosher-for-Passover mustard or hot sauce
1 teaspoon water
1½ cups matzah meal
½ cup almond meal
2 tablespoons sesame seeds (optional)
2 tablespoons dried parsley
1½ teaspoons smoked paprika
1 teaspoon sea salt, plus more for sprinkling
½ teaspoon freshly ground black pepper
2 pounds thinly cut chicken breasts
Vegetable or canola oil for frying

1 Combine the eggs, mustard, and water in a large bowl. Combine the matzah meal, almond meal, sesame seeds (if using), parsley, paprika, salt, and pepper in another large bowl.

2 Dredge each chicken cutlet in the egg mixture, then in the matzah meal mixture, pressing down to ensure the entire piece is covered. Lay flat on a plate or baking sheet.

3 Pour the oil to 1 to 1½ inches' depth into a large sauté pan over medium-high heat.

4 Fry the chicken cutlets in batches, two or three at a time, until golden on each side. Depending on the thickness of the chicken, this will take around 3 minutes per side. Take care not to overcrowd the pan, or the chicken will not cook properly.

5 Remove from the pan and transfer to a wire rack.

6 While the chicken is still hot from the pan, sprinkle each cutlet with an additional pinch of salt.

Baked Cornflake Schnitzel

Serves 4 to 6

Baked cornflake chicken is an American staple, and one that I fell in love with at my "Uncle" David Simkins's house. It's very simple to make, but insanely delicious and comforting. My version of baked cornflake schnitzel uses chicken breasts instead of whole chicken pieces on the bone, and is a little healthier than the version I grew up eating—and kosher-friendly, too. Cornflakes add a nice slightly sweet flavor to the chicken, which also makes it a great dish to serve to kids.

2 pounds boneless skinless chicken cutlets
2 large eggs
1½ teaspoons spicy brown mustard
2 cups cornflake crumbs (around 6 ounces, or half of a 12-ounce box)
1½ teaspoons onion salt
1 teaspoon freshly ground black pepper
½ teaspoon paprika
Cooking spray

1 Preheat the oven to 425°F.

2 Combine the eggs and mustard in a large bowl. Combine the cornflake crumbs, onion salt, pepper, and paprika in another large bowl or shallow baking dish.

3 Dredge each chicken cutlet in the egg mixture, then in the matzah meal mixture, pressing down to ensure the entire piece is covered. Lay flat on a plate or baking sheet.

4 Spray a baking sheet with cooking spray. Place the coated chicken on the baking sheet. Spray the top of the chicken with additional cooking spray.

5 Bake for 15 minutes. Flip over each piece of chicken. Bake for another 7 to 8 minutes, or until the chicken is crisp and slightly browned on both sides, and cooked through.

Notes: **To make the cornflake crumbs, just take cornflake cereal and pulse in a food processor. (Alternatively, place the cornflakes in a resealable plastic bag and use a rolling pin to crush—this is a great task for kids.) You can have some chunks of cornflake and that's fine.**

If you don't have onion salt on hand, you can substitute 2 teaspoons of fine sea salt or table salt.

Corn Schnitzel

Serves 4 to 6

Israelis have a general love of corn: they put it in shakshuka and on top of pizza, and you can even order "corn sticks" at McDonald's in Israel. I once saw a grandma at a playground in Tel Aviv take ears of corn from her purse and present them as snacks for her grandchildren. (It's actually a great idea.) Corn schnitzel may sound like a strange type of schnitzel, since it is more like a patty than thinly pounded meat. However, in Israel, it is popular both as a kid-friendly meal option and as a vegetarian alternative to chicken schnitzel. Serve these corn schnitzel patties with mashed potatoes or rice, and everyone will go home happy.

For the corn patty mixture:

4½ cups (24 ounces) cooked corn (from fresh or frozen)

1 cup bread crumbs

½ cup unbleached all-purpose flour

2 large eggs

1 tablespoon coarsely chopped fresh parsley

1 teaspoon garlic powder

1 teaspoon fine sea salt

½ teaspoon freshly ground black pepper

Bread crumb mixture:

1 cup unseasoned bread crumbs

½ teaspoon fine sea salt

1½ tablespoons sesame seeds

For frying:

Vegetable oil

1 **Make the corn patty mixture:** Pulse the corn in a food processor fitted with the blade attachment until almost smooth but you can still see pieces of corn kernels.

2 Transfer the corn to a bowl and combine with the bread crumbs, flour, eggs, parsley, garlic powder, salt, and pepper.

3 **Make the bread crumb mixture:** In a separate bowl, combine the bread crumbs, salt, and sesame seeds.

4 Form 1-inch-thick round patties of the corn mixture, using around ¼ cup per patty. Dip them into the bread crumb mixture, making sure to press gently so the crumbs stick to the sides. Repeat with all of the corn mixture and the bread crumb mixture.

5 Pour the oil to 1 to 1½ inches' depth into a large sauté pan over medium-high heat.

6 Fry the corn patties until golden brown, around 3 minutes per side.

7 Serve warm with ketchup or other favorite dips.

Zucchini Schnitzel

Serves 4

Zucchini schnitzel is another fun way to make a vegetarian schnitzel, and to use up some of that seasonal, summer zucchini everyone is always wondering what to do with. Serve with lemon wedges and some yogurt tzatziki. You could also try this method using eggplant.

- **2 large zucchini, cut into planks lengthwise (sometimes supermarkets will sell these already prepared)**
- **½ cup all-purpose flour**
- **1½ teaspoons fine sea salt, plus more for sprinkling**
- **¾ teaspoon freshly ground black pepper**
- **2 large eggs, beaten**
- **1 tablespoon water**
- **1 tablespoon spicy brown mustard**
- **1½ cups unseasoned bread crumbs**
- **1 teaspoon onion salt**
- **1 tablespoon dried parsley**
- **2 tablespoons sesame seeds**
- **Vegetable oil for frying**

1 Combine the flour with ½ teaspoon of the salt and ¼ teaspoon of the pepper in a large bowl or shallow baking dish. Whisk together the eggs, water, and mustard in another large bowl or shallow baking dish. Lastly, combine the bread crumbs, remaining teaspoon of salt, remaining ½ teaspoon of pepper, and the onion salt, parsley, and sesame seeds in a third bowl or shallow baking dish.

2 Coat each zucchini piece with the flour mixture, then the egg mixture, and then the bread crumb mixture. Set aside on a baking sheet or large platter.

3 Pour 1 to 1½ inches of oil into large sauté pan over medium-high heat.

4 Fry each breaded slice of zucchini until golden, 3 to 4 minutes on each side.

5 Remove from the pan and transfer to a wire rack. Sprinkle immediately with sea salt.

HORN & HARD

Fish Schnitzel Sandwiches

Serves 4

This dish is my nod to several comfort foods: classic schnitzel, challah, and the iconic McDonald's Filet-O-Fish. Schnitzel is an everyday, home dish and it's not uncommon to find it made with fish in Israel today. For many Jewish American families who kept kosher, the only thing at a McDonald's they might order would be the fish sandwich, and so I know for many American Jews, there is something nostalgic and comforting in that bite of fish sandwich.

My version uses freshly fried fish, homemade challah rolls, tartar sauce, and melted cheese. Get your napkins ready, because it's a messy one, but super comforting and delicious.

For the fish schnitzel:

1 cup all-purpose flour
2 large eggs + 1 tablespoon water
1½ cups panko bread crumbs
2 tablespoons sesame seeds
1 teaspoon sea salt, plus more for sprinkling
½ teaspoon freshly ground black pepper
1 pound white fish, such as flounder, cod, or other thin white fish, cut into sandwich-size pieces (around 6 inches long)
Vegetable oil for frying

For assembly:

Slices of American or Cheddar cheese
Tartar sauce (recipe follows)
1 recipe Small-Batch Challah Rolls (page 75)
Slices of tomato
Shredded iceberg lettuce
Pickle chips

1 **Make the schnitzel:** Place the flour in a shallow baking dish or large bowl. Beat the eggs with the water in a second bowl. Combine the panko bread crumbs, sesame seeds, salt, and pepper in a third bowl.

2 Coat each piece of fish with the flour mixture, then the egg mixture, then the bread crumb mixture. Set aside on a baking sheet or large platter.

3 Pour 1 to 1½ inches of oil into a large sauté pan over medium-high heat.

4 Fry each piece of fish until golden, 3 to 4 minutes on each side. Remove from the pan and transfer to a wire rack. Sprinkle immediately with sea salt.

5 **To assemble each sandwich:** Place a slice of cheese on top of a piece of fish and allow to melt slightly. Spread tartar sauce on each inner side of a sliced challah roll. Place a piece of the cheese-topped fish on the bottom half of the roll and top with sliced tomato, lettuce, and pickle chips, then add the top half of the roll.

SERVE WITH

Tartar Sauce

Makes 1 cup

¼ cup mayonnaise
¼ cup Greek yogurt
Juice of ½ lemon
2 tablespoons chopped cornichons
2 tablespoons chopped fresh dill
¼ teaspoon salt

1 Combine all the ingredients in a small bowl.

2 Store in an airtight container in the refrigerator for up to 1 week.

CHAPTER 6

Meatballs

Let's talk about meatballs.

Every culture has some kind of meatballs, and Jews are no different. From Ashkenazi American sweet-and-sour meatballs to Spanish *albondigas* and North African kebabs, forming ground meat into balls or patties spans cultures and generations. Meatballs were often a way to stretch a little bit of meat into something more substantial, by combining ground meat with eggs, vegetables, and bread crumbs or rice.

Many Sephardic and Mizrahi Jewish meatballs will have rice and vegetables mixed in the meatballs, whereas Ashkenazi meatballs tend to use bread crumbs. Meatballs are adaptable and many of these recipes can be mixed and matched to your taste and dietary needs. If a recipe calls for bread crumbs, you can swap that out for matzah meal or even gluten-free matzah meal. Any way you roll them, they are pure comfort food.

Here are some tips for making meatballs:

- Always make sure to add enough fat and moisture to your meatballs. If you are using a leaner meat, such as chicken or turkey, add an extra tablespoon of oil per pound of meat.
- Don't overwork the meatballs—they can end up tough.
- My standard meatball portions are 1 pound ground meat + 1 large egg + ½ onion + ¼ to ⅓ cup bread crumbs or other binder + seasoning to taste.
- Meatballs are endlessly adaptable, which means you can replace ground beef or lamb with chicken or turkey for a lighter version, and you can add seasoning to your taste.
- You can fry, bake, or simmer meatballs depending on the recipe and your taste. If you choose to bake your meatballs, make sure to spray them with cooking spray on both sides, turn them halfway through cooking, and don't overcook them or they will dry out. Make sure to set a timer, and remove them from the oven as soon as they are slightly browned on both sides.
- Meatballs freeze well, either in sauce or plain. Either freeze meatballs in the sauce (or without) in a resealable plastic freezer bag or a plastic container. They can be frozen for up to 2 months.

Easy Jewish American Sweet-and-Sour Meatballs

Serves 4

The origin of sweet-and-sour meatballs among Jewish Americans is somewhat of a mystery. The sweet-and-sour sauce is similar to that of traditional eastern European stuffed cabbage, but stuffed cabbage is significantly more work than rolling meatballs, and so this may have been a way to more easily adapt the traditional dish.

Sometime in the mid-20th century, a recipe known as "slow cooker meatballs" or "grape jelly meatballs," became popular as an easy and crowd-pleasing appetizer: meatballs were cooked in a mixture of grape jelly and cocktail sauce, and voilà, a new classic was born. Grape jelly and cocktail sauce do have a sweet-and-sour element when combined, and may have also been familiar flavors to American Jews, inspiring them to fully embrace the dish.

Many dishes that were made popular during the 1950s and 1960s were influenced by new products on the market: cream cheese gets added to rugelach dough, cornflakes become a topping for kugel, and onion soup mix becomes a quintessential ingredient for American Jewish brisket. Regardless of its precise origin story, grape jelly sweet-and-sour meatballs are a classic American Jewish dish today, and still a crowd-pleaser. This particular version is inspired by my friends Sarah and Yuval Brokman.

For the meatballs:

1 pound ground beef

1 small onion, finely diced or grated

1 large egg

¼ cup unseasoned bread crumbs

½ teaspoon salt

¼ teaspoon freshly ground black pepper

¼ teaspoon garlic powder

For the sauce:

One 12-ounce bottled chili sauce, ketchup, or tomato sauce

¼ cup grape jelly

¼ cup raisins

1 cup chicken or vegetable stock

1 **Make the meatballs:** Combine the ground beef, onion, and egg in a bowl. In a separate bowl, mix together the bread crumbs, salt, pepper, and garlic powder.

2 Add the bread crumb mixture to the meat mixture and mix until just combined, taking care not to overmix. Keeping a small bowl of cold water next to you, roll the meatball mixture into walnut-size balls, using the palm of your hands, dipping your hands into the cold water before forming each ball.

3 **Make the sauce:** Combine all the sauce ingredients in a medium-large saucepan and bring to a simmer. Add the meatballs to the sauce and cook, covered, over medium-low heat for 45 minutes.

Sweet-and-Sour Meatballs

in Tomato Sauce

Serves 4

This recipe relies more on vegetables and canned tomatoes to season the sauce, making this dish a bit healthier than the grape jelly and cocktail sauce version, but no less delicious. We love serving these meatballs with egg noodles or rice, and replace the bread crumbs with matzah meal during Passover.

For the sauce:

2 tablespoons olive oil
1 medium onion, finely diced
2 garlic cloves, minced
One 28-ounce can crushed tomatoes
¼ cup light brown sugar
Juice of 1 lemon or ⅓ cup apple cider vinegar
1 cup water or chicken or beef broth
¼ teaspoon ground cinnamon
½ teaspoon salt
¼ teaspoon freshly ground black pepper

For the meatballs:

⅓ cup unseasoned bread crumbs or matzah meal
¼ teaspoon fresh cinnamon
¼ teaspoon ground ginger or ½ teaspoon finely minced fresh
½ teaspoon salt
¼ teaspoon freshly ground black pepper
1 pound ground beef
1 large egg
½ onion, grated or finely diced

1 **Make the sauce:** Heat the olive oil in a large saucepan over medium-high heat. Cook the onion for 7 to 8 minutes, until soft and translucent. Add the garlic and cook for another 2 minutes. Add the crushed tomatoes, brown sugar, lemon juice, cinnamon, salt, and pepper. Bring to a simmer and then cook over low heat while preparing the meatballs.

2 **Make the meatballs:** Mix together the bread crumbs, cinnamon, ginger, salt, and pepper in a bowl. In a separate bowl, combine the ground beef, egg, and onion.

3 Add the bread crumb mixture to the meat mixture and mix until just combined, taking care not to overmix. Keeping a small bowl of cold water next to you, roll the meatball mixture into walnut-size balls, using the palm of your hands, dipping your hands into the cold water before forming each ball.

4 Place all the meatballs in the sauce and simmer, covered, over medium-low heat for 45 to 50 minutes.

Chicken Meatballs

with Lemon Garlic Sauce

Serves 4

Sometimes chicken or turkey meatballs can be tough or dry. But frying these meatballs and serving them in a lemony sauce retains their moisture and provides tons of flavor.

For the meatballs:

1 large egg, lightly beaten

½ cup grated onion (about 1 small onion, or ½ large)

2 garlic cloves, minced

1 tablespoon grated lemon zest

1 tablespoon fresh lemon juice

1 pound ground chicken

½ cup unseasoned bread crumbs

½ teaspoon salt

¼ teaspoon freshly ground black pepper

½ teaspoon dried oregano

Vegetable oil for frying

For the sauce:

1 tablespoon olive oil

1 small onion, sliced into half-moons

2 garlic cloves, minced

Leaves from a few thyme sprigs

1 cup white wine or Chicken Stock (page 14)

Juice of 1 lemon

¼ teaspoon salt

¼ teaspoon freshly ground black pepper

1 **Make the meatballs:** Combine the egg, grated onion, garlic, and lemon zest and juice in a medium bowl. Add the ground chicken and mix to combine.

2 In a separate bowl, combine the bread crumbs with the salt, pepper, and oregano.

3 Combine the bread crumb mixture with the meat mixture until just mixed, but take care not to overmix. Keeping a small bowl of cold water next to you, roll the meatball mixture into walnut-size balls, using the palm of your hands, dipping your hands into the cold water before forming each ball.

4 Heat a few tablespoons of vegetable oil in a large skillet over medium heat. Fry the meatballs in batches, turning until golden on all sides and cooked through, 3 to 4 minutes per batch depending on the size of your meatballs. If you aren't sure, go ahead and cut into one to make sure it's cooked through. As you fry the meatballs, you may need to add a little extra oil to the pan. Remove from the pan when cooked.

5 **Make the sauce:** Using the same pan in which you sautéed the meatballs, heat the olive oil. Add the sliced onion and sauté until translucent, around 7 minutes. Add the garlic and thyme and cook for another 2 minutes. Add the wine, lemon juice, salt, and pepper, scraping any bits off the bottom of the pan. Reduce the sauce slightly, cooking for 2 to 3 minutes. Add the meatballs back to the pan and coat with the sauce.

recipe continues

SERVE WITH

Creamy Zucchini Israeli Couscous

Serves 4

Israeli couscous, also known as *ptitim*, isn't couscous at all, but pasta that is shaped like tiny pearls, which is why you will also see it called "pearl couscous." Israeli couscous was invented in the aftermath of Israel's War of Independence, when the country was forced to ration food, and Prime Minister David Ben-Gurion asked the food company Osem to create a more affordable starch as an alternative to rice. The pasta became a staple and remains a popular comfort food today.

Most recipes call for toasting ptitim first before cooking the pasta in water or broth. If you don't have Israeli couscous, you could substitute orzo pasta.

2 tablespoons olive oil
1 shallot or small onion, diced
2 garlic cloves, minced
8 ounces uncooked Israeli couscous or orzo pasta
Leaves from a few thyme sprigs
1 zucchini, grated
2½ to 3 cups Chicken Stock (page 14)
½ teaspoon fine sea salt
¼ teaspoon freshly ground black pepper
2 teaspoons grated lemon zest
Fresh parsley, dill, or chives (optional)

1 Heat a large skillet over medium-high heat. Add the olive oil and shallot and cook until the shallot is translucent, 4 to 5 minutes. Add the garlic and cook for another 2 minutes.

2 Stir in the Israeli couscous and thyme and cook until golden and toasted, 2 to 3 minutes. Stir in the zucchini and cook for another 1 to 2 minutes.

3 Add ½ cup of the stock and deglaze the pan. Add another 2 cups of stock and simmer over medium-low heat, constantly stirring. Add the salt and pepper.

4 Simmer for 8 to 10 minutes, stirring constantly, until the Israeli couscous is al dente, adding more stock if needed. Serve with fresh lemon zest and more fresh herbs, if desired.

Lamb Meatballs

with Two Sauces

Serves 6 to 8

Throughout the Middle East and many parts of Europe, lamb is a very common meat. Personally, I love lamb in many forms, and these meatballs have a nice amount of warmth and spice without being overpowering. This is also the kind of recipe that you can add more, or less, spice depending on your taste.

I like serving these meatballs several different ways. For a saucy version, simmer them in this spiced harissa tomato sauce. Another option is to fry or bake them and then to serve with herbed tahini sauce. You could also serve these on top of shakshuka or hummus.

For the meatballs:

2 pounds ground lamb
1 onion, grated
3 tablespoons minced fresh mint
3 tablespoons minced fresh flat-leaf parsley
2 garlic cloves, minced
2 large eggs
1 teaspoon salt
½ teaspoon ground cumin
¼ teaspoon freshly ground black pepper
Vegetable or another neutral oil for frying

For the harissa tomato sauce:

1 to 2 tablespoons olive oil
1 onion, finely diced
2 garlic cloves
Pinch of caraway seeds
2 tablespoons tomato paste
One 28-ounce can diced tomatoes
One 28-ounce can crushed tomatoes
3 heaping tablespoons harissa paste
1½ cups water or Chicken Stock (page 14)
½ teaspoon salt
¼ teaspoon freshly ground black pepper

For the herbed tahini sauce:

½ cup good-quality tahini
⅓ cup ice water, or more
Juice of ½ lemon
⅓ cup chopped fresh herbs, such as dill, cilantro, parsley, and/or mint
½ teaspoon salt
¼ teaspoon freshly ground black pepper

1 **Make the meatballs:** Combine the ground lamb, mint, parsley, garlic, eggs, salt, cumin, and pepper in a large bowl. Using your hands, mix until combined throughout, but take care not to overwork the meat.

2 Form tablespoon-size meatballs, using your hands or a cookie scoop. Roll gently and place on a plate until ready to fry.

3 Heat vegetable oil in a large sauté pan over medium heat. Fry the meatballs in batches until browned, rotating them to ensure they have been browned on all sides.

4 Remove from the pan. You may need to add a little more oil in between batches.

5 **Make the harissa tomato sauce:** Heat the olive oil in a large pot over medium-high heat. Sauté the onion until translucent and soft, 7 to 10 minutes. Add the garlic, a pinch of caraway seeds, and tomato paste, and sauté for another 2 minutes.

6 Add the diced and crushed tomatoes, harissa or stock, and water and bring to a low simmer. Cook, covered, for 30 to 40 minutes over low heat. The tomato sauce is done when the tomatoes have broken down and the sauce has reduced slightly.

7 **Make the herbed tahini sauce:** Place the tahini in a small bowl. Add the ⅓ cup of ice water slowly, while whisking. Keep adding water while whisking until a smooth consistency is reached. Don't worry if the tahini seems as if it is too thick at first—just keep drizzling in the cold water and it will smooth out.

8 Add the lemon juice, herbs, salt, and pepper. Taste and adjust the seasoning.

North African Chraime Fish Patties

Serves 4

For Americans, the idea of fish balls may seem strange in its name, but that's exactly what gefilte fish is: fish patties. In Israel, simmered fish patties, or balls, is a very common dish. One of the most beloved dishes for Moroccan Jews is *chraime*, which is white fish filets simmered in a spiced tomato sauce. But many next-generation Israelis and Israeli Americans I know have adapted this beloved dish and changed the fish patties into balls. They are most often served as a Shabbat main dish, and I think the contrast of the fresh green herbs, the white flesh of the fish, and the tomato sauce all create an incredibly striking dish for any celebratory table.

For the fish patties:

1 pound meaty white fish, such as cod, halibut, or flounder, finely chopped

1 onion, grated

1 garlic clove, minced

1 large egg

2 tablespoons chopped fresh cilantro

⅓ cup bread crumbs

½ teaspoon fine sea salt

For the sauce:

2 tablespoons olive oil

1 small white onion, diced

1 jalapeño pepper, seeded and diced

2 garlic cloves, minced

1 lemon, trimmed, seeded, and diced

¼ cup tomato paste

4 fresh beefsteak (Jersey) tomatoes, chopped, or one 28-ounce can diced tomatoes

½ teaspoon caraway seeds

1 teaspoon ground cumin

1 teaspoon ground turmeric

1 teaspoon ground coriander

½ teaspoon ground Aleppo pepper or red pepper flakes

½ teaspoon sugar or honey

Fresh cilantro for serving

1 **Make the fish patties:** Combine the fish, grated onion, garlic, egg, cilantro, and bread crumbs in a medium bowl. Place in the fridge to chill for 1 to 2 hours.

2 After the fish has chilled, fill a small bowl with cool water. Using the palm of your hands, roll the fish into walnut-size patties or balls, dipping your hands into the water before forming each patty or ball. Place them on a plate and back in the fridge until ready to add to the sauce.

3 **Make the sauce:** Heat the olive oil in a sauté pan over medium heat. Sauté the diced onion for 7 to 10 minutes, until translucent. Add the jalapeño and garlic and cook for 2 to 3 minutes. Add the diced lemon and tomato paste and cook for another 2 to 3 minutes.

4 Add the fresh or canned tomatoes, caraway seeds, cumin, turmeric, coriander, Aleppo pepper, and sugar. Cook over medium-low heat for 10 to 15 minutes, until the tomatoes start to break down.

5 Add the fish patties to the sauce and cook for 15 minutes.

6 Top with fresh cilantro for serving. Serve with rice or couscous.

Notes: **In this recipe, make sure you chop up the fish extremely finely. If you don't, the patties won't hold together well.**

You will chop up an entire lemon, skin and all, for the sauce. Just make sure to remove any seeds.

Chickpea Cauliflower "Meatballs"

Serves 4 to 6

Chickpeas play a central role in a lot of Israeli and Middle Eastern cooking, being a cheap source of vegetarian protein. These "meatballs" made with ground chickpeas and cauliflower are the perfect vegetarian alternative to meat-based meatballs and can be paired with any of the sauces in this chapter.

2 cups cauliflower rice (see Note)
2 cups canned chickpeas, drained and rinsed
1 medium onion, grated
2 large eggs
1½ tablespoons soy sauce
2 tablespoons olive oil
1 cup bread crumbs or matzah meal
1 teaspoon onion salt or fine sea salt
½ teaspoon freshly ground black pepper
Cooking spray

1 Preheat the oven to 400°F. Line a baking sheet with parchment paper.

2 Combine the cauliflower rice and chickpeas in a food processor fitted with a blade. Pulse for 1 minute, or until the mixture comes together. If you prefer a chunkier mixture, pulse a little less.

3 Transfer the pulsed mixture to a bowl. Add the onion, egg, soy sauce, olive oil, bread crumbs, onion salt, and pepper.

4 Roll the mixture into walnut-size "meatballs."

5 Spray the prepared baking sheet with cooking spray. Place the meatballs on top of the parchment, and then spray the meatballs with additional cooking spray.

6 Bake for 15 minutes. Turn over the meatballs and spray again with more cooking spray. Bake for another 7 to 10 minutes, until golden and slightly crispy on both sides.

7 Remove from the oven and allow to cool. Combine with the sauce of your choice.

Note: **You can find cauliflower rice in most supermarkets in the frozen section, and many stores will carry fresh cauliflower rice in the produce section as well. I like keeping bags of frozen cauliflower in my freezer for last-minute easy lunches or dinners. But you can also just break up one head of cauliflower for this recipe and add it to the food processor with the chickpeas.**

My Mom's Italian American Meatballs

Serves 6 to 8

Many Jewish families in America, Israel, and around the world make Italian American–style spaghetti and meatballs regularly. It is a pretty universally loved dish. But you are unlikely to find spaghetti, meatballs, and tomato sauce on any restaurant menus in the actual country of Italy.

Meatballs in Italy, known as *polpette*, are typically smaller and served without sauce. Italian immigrants who came to the United States in the late 19th and early 20th centuries (a similar time frame when many European Jewish immigrants were also arriving in the United States) found meat in abundance and cheaper than in Italy. Pairing it with dried pasta and canned tomatoes they turned into sauce, it was a filling meal at a time when they needed to stretch food a little further. This story of culinary transformation can be found across many immigrant groups; it is the story of how a people adapts in new places, adopting new foods, and creating something that both connects them to their past, yet is something beautiful and new.

I grew up frying meatballs with my own Italian mom in our upstate New York home. She taught me to fry a little piece of the meatball mixture before moving on to fry the whole batch; this way, you can taste and make sure the seasoning is right. After all, you can always add more salt or spices, but you can't take them away if you add too much.

My mom always fried her meatballs, then finished cooking them in her homemade tomato sauce. I never had the chance to learn her exact recipe, because she passed away from cancer when I was a teenager, but these are as close as I can re-create, and I always feel a sense of pride when my husband, friends, or children ask me to make a batch.

recipe continues

For the tomato sauce:

2 tablespoons olive oil

1 onion, finely diced

2 medium carrots, peeled and shredded

3 garlic cloves, minced

Two 28-ounce cans crushed tomatoes

½ cup dry red wine

1 teaspoon sugar

2 tablespoons balsamic vinegar

Handful of fresh basil leaves

Salt and freshly ground black pepper

For the meatballs:

2 pounds ground beef

2 large eggs

2 tablespoons minced fresh garlic

1 onion, grated

½ cup unseasoned bread crumbs

½ teaspoon dried basil

¼ teaspoon dried oregano

3 tablespoons chopped fresh parsley

1 teaspoon fine sea salt

¼ teaspoon freshly ground black pepper

For frying:

Vegetable oil

Olive oil

1 **Make the sauce:** Add the olive oil to a large saucepan over medium-high heat. Cook the onion and carrots until the onion is soft and translucent, around 8 minutes. Add the garlic and cook for another 2 minutes. Add the crushed tomatoes, red wine, sugar, balsamic vinegar, and fresh basil. Bring to a simmer over medium heat and cook for at least 30 minutes while you prepare the meatballs.

2 **Make the meatballs:** Place the ground meat, eggs, garlic, and onion in a large bowl and mix gently with your hands. In a separate bowl, combine the bread crumbs, dried basil, oregano, parsley, salt, and pepper and mix well.

3 Mix the bread crumb mixture and the meat mixture until just combined, taking care not to overmix. Keeping a small bowl of cold water next to you, roll the meatball mixture into walnut-size balls, using the palm of your hands, dipping your hands into cold water before forming each ball.

4 **To fry:** Heat a few tablespoons (around 2) of vegetable oil and a few tablespoons of olive oil in a large sauté pan over medium-high heat. Fry the meatballs in batches, turning on all sides, until a nice golden-brown crust forms. Remove from the pan and place on a plate lined with a paper towel. Repeat until all the meatballs have been fried. You may need to add additional oil as you fry. It's okay if the meatballs aren't cooked all the way through at this stage; they will finish cooking in the sauce.

5 Place all the meatballs in the sauce and simmer, covered, over low heat for 50 to 60 minutes.

6 Before serving remove the whole basil leaves.

7 Serve the meatballs and sauce over your preferred pasta.

Notes: **If you prefer not to fry the meatballs, you can bake them in a 375°F oven for 20 to 25 minutes, turning once so they get slightly browned on both sides. Remove from the oven and then add to the simmering sauce.**

To make an extra-rich sauce, you could also add a few marrow bones, a 1- to 2-pound piece of chuck roast, or Italian-style sausages to the sauce once it is simmering.

CHAPTER 7

Dumplings and Pastries

Let's talk about dumplings.

Every culture has their own version of a dumpling or savory pastry; Italian cuisine has ravioli. Argentineans have empanadas, and within Jewish cuisine, there is an incredible diversity of dumplings and savory pastries.

Ashkenazi kreplach are perhaps the most well-known dumplings for American Jewry, but they are far from the only variety. Persian Jews enjoy *gondi*, a cross between a dumpling and a meatball, which is made with chickpea flour and ground chicken and served in soup. Another Jewish dumpling served in soup is Iraqi kubeh, which is made with semolina flour, filled with meat, and traditionally served in red broth that is made with beets or in a green version known as *hamousta*, which is made with greens and lemon.

Whereas kreplach, gondi, and kubeh are all served simmered in broth, Ashkenazi knishes and Israeli *bourekas* are more like hand pockets: easily portable, cheap, and filling street food that can be made innumerable ways. In Israel, you can find bourekas anywhere—every *makolet* (small market) will have a selection to grab on the go. On the streets of New York City, hot dog carts often have knishes, too—a cheap way to have a quick bite. Bourekas were popularized in Israel by Jews from Turkey and the Balkans. The most traditional fillings of these flaky pastries are cheese, spinach, potato, and mushroom; you can find knishes in many of the same varieties at delis around North America.

Sambousek are Syrian pastries, which are most commonly filled with cheese and shaped similarly to an empanada, with beautifully crimped edges. Whereas Argentinean empanadas are made with a wheat flour dough, Syrian sambousek are made with semolina flour.

In this chapter, I am sharing a few of my own favorites, which span Ashkenazi, Georgian, Syrian, and Jewish American traditions, but there are so many more dumplings and pastries to explore.

Here are a few tips for making these dumplings and pastries from scratch:

- Take care not to overstuff dumplings or pastries, otherwise the filling is likely to seep or explode out.
- Ensuring the dough is the right consistency is essential, and the doughs do vary, so pay attention to the recipes.
- As with any kind of recipe that includes flour and water, the exact amounts of each may change depending on where you live and the time of year. So, getting to know what the dough should ideally feel like is important.
- You absolutely can freeze dumplings and savory pastries, but unlike other dishes, such as stuffed cabbage, you want to freeze them before you cook them. You can then boil or bake them straight from the freezer.

CLASSIC

Meat Kreplach

Makes 2 dozen dumplings

I was extremely intimidated to try my hand at kreplach before my friend and fellow cookbook author Ronnie Fein taught me many years ago. I didn't grow up eating kreplach, and most American Jewish cooks don't make kreplach from scratch anymore, instead opting to use wonton wrappers, so homemade dumplings felt like a monumental task. But kreplach are somewhat forgiving, being a quintessential home-cooked dish. They don't have to look perfect; in fact, having a bit of rustic-ness in the shape adds to their charm.

Kreplach dough is not any different from a traditional flour-based pasta dough. I highly recommend using a pasta roller, if you have one; it will make the task of getting a thin dough much easier. If not, just some good old-fashioned elbow grease and a rolling pin will work fine. My preferred filling is cooked chuck roast, as it has good flavor and a bit of fat. But you can also use ground beef, chopped-up brisket, or even a meat alternative, such as Impossible Meat.

The best way to freeze kreplach is to fill and shape them, and then lay them in a single layer on a baking sheet. Place it in the freezer, and when they are completely frozen, transfer the frozen kreplach to resealable plastic freezer bags. When ready to cook, remove from the bags and place in boiling water to heat for around 20 minutes.

For the dough:

2 cups unbleached all-purpose flour, plus more for dusting

½ teaspoon fine sea salt

3 large eggs

2 tablespoons vegetable oil

For the filling:

2 cups cooked chuck roast (around 12 ounces; page 125)

1 large egg

1 teaspoon paprika

1 **Make the dough by hand:** Combine the flour and salt in a large bowl. Create a well in the middle and add the eggs and oil. Knead until the dough is smooth.

2 **Alternatively, make the dough in a food processor:** Combine all the dough ingredients in a food processor. Pulse until the dough comes together, pulling away from the sides of the bowl.

3 Wrap the dough in plastic wrap and allow it to rest in the fridge for 1 hour. You can prepare the dough a day in advance.

4 **Make the filling:** Finely chop the meat and combine with the egg and paprika in a medium bowl.

5 Divide the dough into two portions, and keep the remaining piece of dough covered while rolling out the first. Using a pasta roller or rolling pin, roll them into thin sheets, as thin as you can get.

6 Cut the dough into approximately 3-inch squares. Place around 1 teaspoon of filling in the middle of one square. Using your finger, dab the edges of the square with water and fold into a triangle, sealing the edges with your fingers or a fork. Repeat with the remaining dough and filling.

7 Place the kreplach on a lightly floured baking sheet and set aside until ready to cook.

8 At this point, you can bring a large pot of salted water to a simmer. Add the kreplach and simmer for 12 to 15 minutes.

Turn Kreplach Dough into Noodles

This kreplach dough can be used to make egg noodles for soup or other noodle dishes. Follow the directions to make the dough and let it rest. Divide the dough into four equal pieces. Cover the remaining pieces with a clean dish towel while you work with one. Start by shaping one of the pieces of dough into a flattened oval or rectangular shape with your hands.

Run the piece of dough two times through the widest setting of a pasta maker. Repeat on the next two settings until you have thin rectangular sheets. Repeat the entire process with the other pieces of dough. At this point, you can loosely fold each thin sheet of dough into an accordion, and then cut into strips.

Alternatively, you can feed sheets of dough through the fettuccine pasta attachment.

Dust the pasta lightly with flour and lay onto a baking sheet until ready to cook. Boil in salted water for 3 to 5 minutes.

Red Wine–Braised Chuck Roast

Serves 4 to 6

Brisket is a staple for Ashkenazi American Jews, dating back to Europe at a time when it was considered a less desirable cut, and so cheaper. But I actually prefer chuck roast or pot roast over a brisket. I find it more flavorful and tender, and maybe even a smidge more forgiving. You don't have to slice it against the grain in a specific way, and it's so easy in a slow cooker.

For more heft, you can add around 2 pounds of mini red potatoes to the pot or slow cooker halfway through the cooking time, so the potatoes and meat are finished cooking at the same time.

To cook in a slow cooker, follow steps 1 through 5 of the following instructions. Place all the ingredients in the slow cooker on LOW for 8 hours, or HIGH for 4 hours.

One 3- to 4-pound chuck roast
Salt and freshly ground black pepper
2 to 3 tablespoons neutral oil
3 carrots, rough chopped
3 celery stalks, rough chopped
2 garlic cloves
2 tablespoons tomato paste
2 teaspoons onion salt or other seasoned salt
½ teaspoon freshly ground black pepper
4 cups water, Chicken Stock (page 14), or a combination of both
Half 750-milliliter bottle red wine

1 Pat the chuck roast dry on all sides, using paper towels. Season all over with salt and pepper.

2 Heat the oil in a large Dutch oven or large heavy-bottomed pot over medium-high heat.

3 Sear the chuck roast on all sides until a golden-brown crust forms, 4 to 5 minutes on each side. Remove from the pan and set aside, then lower the heat to medium.

4 Pour off all but about 2 tablespoons of the rendered fat into a heatproof bowl. When cool, discard the bowlful of fat.

5 Add the onion, carrots, and celery to the fat remaining in the same Dutch oven or pot. Sauté over medium heat until softened, 6 to 7 minutes. Add the garlic and tomato paste and cook for another 2 minutes, or until combined.

6 Add the water or stock, red wine, onion salt or other seasoning, and pepper. Bring to a low boil, then return the chuck roast and all its juices to the pot.

7 Lower the heat to low and cover the pot. Cook for 3 to 4 hours, until the meat is completely tender. Check periodically to ensure the heat isn't too high. When the meat is easily shredded, it's done cooking. Season with salt to taste.

Corned Beef and Cabbage Kreplach

Makes 2 dozen kreplach

The story of how corned beef and cabbage became known as an Irish dish in America is one of my favorite Jewish food stories. In such neighborhoods as the Lower East Side, and in Brooklyn and the Bronx, multiple immigrant groups, including Jewish, Italian, and Irish, all lived next to one another, influencing countless dishes and food choices.

It was at Jewish delis and street carts in the late 19th and early 20th centuries that Irish immigrants noticed Jewish corned beef and thought it looked and tasted similar to the bacon back in Ireland. Bacon and cabbage served together was a traditional Irish dish, but at that time, bacon wasn't as widely available or affordable, and so Irish immigrants could replace the bacon with corned beef. Cooking corned beef with the cabbage also made preparation for the dish easier, since it could all be done in one pot. And so corned beef and cabbage was born out of necessity, but also became its own uniquely Jewish-Irish-American culinary expression.

This dish is a playful version of kreplach made with mashed potato, corned beef, and sautéed cabbage. I suggest frying these kreplach after they are boiled, but you could also serve them without frying.

For the dough:

2 cups unbleached all-purpose flour, plus more for dusting
½ teaspoon fine sea salt
3 large eggs
2 tablespoons vegetable oil

For the filling:

1 russet potato, peeled and diced
4 to 5 tablespoons olive oil
1 large onion, diced
2 cups shredded cabbage, chopped
4 ounces sliced corned beef, finely diced
1 large egg
¼ teaspoon garlic powder
½ teaspoon salt

Spicy brown mustard for serving (optional)

1 **Make the dough by hand:** Combine the flour and fine sea salt in a large bowl. Create a well in the middle and add the eggs and vegetable oil. Knead until the dough is smooth.

2 **Alternatively, make the dough in a food processor:** Combine all the dough ingredients in a food processor. Pulse until the dough comes together, pulling away from the sides of the bowl.

3 Wrap the dough in plastic wrap and allow it to rest in the fridge for 1 hour. You can prepare the dough a day in advance.

4 **Make the filling:** Bring a small saucepan of salted water to a boil. Add the potato and cook until tender, 10 to 12 minutes. You can tell the potato is done when you can easily insert a fork into it.

5 Heat 2 to 3 tablespoons of the olive oil in a large sauté pan over medium heat. Add the onion and cook for 5 to 6 minutes, until slightly translucent and soft. Add the chopped cabbage and continue to cook until completely cooked and wilted.

6 Mash the potato in a large bowl. Add the cabbage mixture, corned beef, egg, garlic powder, and salt and combine.

7 Divide the dough into two portions, and keep the remaining piece of dough covered while rolling out the first. Using a pasta roller or rolling pin, roll into thin sheets, as thin as you can get.

8 Cut the dough into approximately 3-inch squares. Place around 1 teaspoon of filling in the middle of one square. Using your finger, dab the edges of the square with water and fold into a triangle, sealing the edges with your fingers or a fork. Repeat with the remaining dough and filling.

9 Place the kreplach on a lightly floured baking sheet and set aside until ready to cook.

10 At this point, you can bring a large pot of salted water to a simmer. Add the kreplach and simmer for 12 to 15 minutes.

11 Once the kreplach have cooked, add the remaining 2 tablespoons of olive oil to a large sauté pan over medium heat. Fry the kreplach until golden on each side.

12 Serve with spicy brown mustard, if desired.

Thanksgiving Turkey Kreplach

Makes 2 dozen kreplach

Kreplach are one of the many Jewish foods that were created as a way to take a little bit of meat and to make it stretch into a fuller dish. I find that, at Thanksgiving, there's always a bit of turkey left over from the holiday. Turkey-filled kreplach is a perfect way to use up that bit of extra meat and to turn it into something more exciting than just leftovers. If you also have some mashed potatoes, you could add that to the filling as well.

For the kreplach dough:

2 cups unbleached all-purpose flour, plus more for dusting

½ teaspoon fine sea salt

3 large eggs

2 tablespoons vegetable oil

For the filling:

2 cups leftover turkey (a mixture of white and dark meat is fine)

1 large egg

1 teaspoon fresh thyme leaves

Salt and freshly ground black pepper

1 **Make the dough by hand:** Combine the flour and fine sea salt in a large bowl. Create a well in the middle and add the eggs and oil. Knead until the dough is smooth.

2 **Alternatively, make the dough in a food processor:** Combine all the dough ingredients in a food processor. Pulse until the dough comes together, pulling away from the sides of the bowl.

3 Wrap the dough in plastic wrap and allow it to rest in the fridge for 1 hour. You can prepare the dough a day in advance.

4 **Make the filling:** Finely chop the turkey meat. Place it in a medium bowl and combine with the egg, thyme, and salt and pepper to taste. Set aside.

5 Divide the dough into two portions, and keep the remaining piece of dough covered while rolling out the first. Using a pasta roller or rolling pin, roll into thin sheets, as thin as you can get.

6 Cut the dough into approximately 3-inch squares. Place around 1 teaspoon of filling in the middle of one square. Using your finger, dab the edges of the square with water and fold into a triangle, sealing the edges with your fingers or a fork. Repeat with the remaining dough and filling.

7 Place the kreplach on a lightly floured baking sheet and set aside until ready to cook.

8 At this point, you can bring a large pot of salted water to a simmer. Add the kreplach and simmer for 12 to 15 minutes.

9 Serve in turkey stock (recipe follows) or other homemade soup.

SERVE WITH

Turkey Stock

Serves 6 to 8

I think most Americans can agree that the best part of Thanksgiving is the leftovers. In my family, my dad always made turkey noodle soup the day after Thanksgiving with the leftover turkey carcass. Fast forward, and I do the same thing. You can make this rich broth and serve simply with egg noodles, or even matzah balls. But another fun thing to do is to serve the turkey kreplach in the turkey stock itself, doing the ultimate Jewish thing: using every part of the animal.

1 to 2 leftover turkey carcasses
1 large onion
4 large carrots, peeled and cut into chunks
4 celery stalks, cut into chunks
2 parsnips, peeled and cut into chunks
1 bunch of parsley
A few thyme sprigs
1 bay leaf
1 tablespoon whole peppercorns
Salt and freshly ground black pepper

1 Place all the ingredients, except the salt and pepper, in a large stockpot and cover with cold water. Bring to a boil and then lower the heat to medium.

2 Simmer for 2 hours, skimming the top of the soup to remove fat and any scum that rises to the top.

3 Remove the turkey carcass and vegetables, and reserve the vegetables. Simmer the soup again over medium-low heat for another 30 to 45 minutes, until the stock has reduced just slightly and the flavor is rich.

4 Season with salt and pepper to taste.

5 Serve with the reserved vegetables, diced leftover turkey meat, cooked kreplach, egg noodles, and matzah balls, if desired.

Sweet Cheese Kreplach

Makes 2 dozen dumplings

These sweet cheese kreplach taste very similar to blintzes, and are beloved by my middle daughter. I serve these just like blintzes or cheese pancakes, with powdered sugar and a bit of jam. They are perfect for the Jewish holiday of Shavuot, when it is traditional to enjoy dairy foods, but are also delicious for brunch anytime.

For the dough:

2 cups unbleached all-purpose flour, plus more for dusting
½ teaspoon fine sea salt
3 large eggs
2 tablespoons vegetable oil

For the filling:

7½ ounces farmer (pot) cheese
4 ounces full-fat cream cheese or goat cheese
¼ cup granulated sugar
½ teaspoon vanilla extract
1 to 2 teaspoons orange zest

For frying:

1 tablespoon olive oil
1 tablespoon unsalted butter

For serving:

Powdered sugar
Jam

Note: **This recipe calls for using one 7½-ounce package of farmer cheese. You can typically find farmer cheese near the cream cheese in major supermarket chains. If you cannot find it, you could substitute fresh ricotta.**

1 **Make the dough by hand:** Combine the flour and salt in a large bowl. Create a well in the middle and add the eggs and oil. Knead until the dough is smooth.

2 **Alternatively, make the dough in a food processor:** Combine all the dough ingredients in a food processor. Pulse until the dough comes together, pulling away from the sides of the bowl.

3 Wrap the dough in plastic wrap and allow it to rest in the fridge for 1 hour. You can prepare the dough a day in advance.

4 **Make the filling:** Combine the farmer cheese, cream cheese, granulated sugar, vanilla, and orange zest in a medium bowl. Set aside.

5 Divide the dough into two portions, and keep the remaining piece of dough covered while rolling out the first. Using a pasta roller or rolling pin, roll into thin sheets, as thin as you can get.

6 Cut the dough into approximately 3-inch squares. Place around 1 teaspoon of filling in the middle of one square. Using your finger, dab the edges of the square with water and fold into a triangle, sealing the edges with your fingers or a fork. Repeat with the remaining dough and filling.

7 Place the kreplach on a lightly floured baking sheet and set aside until ready to cook.

8 At this point, you can bring a large pot of salted water to a simmer. Add the kreplach and simmer for 12 to 15 minutes.

9 Once the kreplach have cooked, heat the olive oil and butter in a large sauté pan. Fry the kreplach until golden on each side.

10 Serve with powdered sugar and jam.

Georgian Meat Khinkali

Makes 20 dumplings

If eastern European kreplach and Shanghai *xia long bao* had a baby somewhere on the spice trail in between, it would be Georgian *khinkali*. Khinkali are Georgian dumplings said to have originated in the mountains outside Tbilisi. But we know that Georgian cuisine, because of its geography, is heavily influenced by the foods and flavors of Russia, Iran, Turkey, and China, too, which surely inspired these delectable dumplings.

The shape of khinkali, with their signature pleats at the top, is more similar to their Chinese counterpart than perhaps an eastern European-style kreplach, and the filling is quite souplike, with a bit of extra broth to slurp up, which is part of the fun of eating these. Unlike xia long bao, khinkali have a signature handle.

Khinkali are most traditionally filled with a mixture of beef and pork, but can also be filled with potato, cheese, or mushrooms. They are just a tad spicy, and absolutely addictive, with their brothy, meaty contents spilling into your mouth with each messy bite. Traditionally, you aren't supposed to eat the handle, but actually leave the little dough nubs on your plate so you can go back and count how many you have eaten. The handle also tends to be a little tough and doesn't have any meat inside, so it makes sense not to eat it.

These dumplings do take a bit of practice to make, especially creating those pleats, so do not despair if they don't come out perfect the first try. Look up some videos on YouTube. Have fun with it. No matter what they look like, I promise they will be delicious. If you end up with extra filling, roll it into meatballs and bake or fry them for a snack.

For the dough:

2½ cups unbleached all-purpose flour
½ teaspoon salt
1 cup lukewarm water
Cooking spray for bowl

For the filling:

8 ounces ground beef
8 ounces ground veal
½ large onion, grated or very finely diced
2 tablespoons chopped fresh parsley
2 tablespoons chopped fresh cilantro
1 teaspoon fine sea salt
½ teaspoon smoked paprika
¼ to ⅓ teaspoon red pepper flakes
½ cup cool water

For serving:

Freshly ground black pepper
Chopped fresh dill

1 **Make the dough:** Combine the flour, salt, and lukewarm water in a stand mixer fitted with a dough hook. Mix until smooth. Place the dough in a bowl that has been greased with cooking spray, cover with a clean, damp towel or plastic wrap, and allow it to rest for 30 minutes.

2 **Make the filling:** Combine the beef and veal, onion, parsley, cilantro, salt, paprika, and red pepper flakes in a medium bowl. Slowly add the cool water until incorporated. The mixture should feel a little bit wet. Place in the fridge until ready to use.

3 After the dough has rested for 30 minutes, remove it from the bowl and knead for another 5 minutes, or until totally smooth. Divide the dough in half, covering half of the dough to keep it from drying out.

4 Roll the dough into a snakelike shape and begin to portion off walnut-size pieces. Using a rolling pin, roll each piece of dough into a disk around 6 inches in diameter.

5 Place one dough disk on a small dessert plate with a slight rim.

6 Spoon around ¼ cup of the filling onto the middle of the disk.

recipe continues

7 Pull up one edge of the dough and bring it toward the center. Using your middle finger and thumb, make a few pleats, and then turn the plate by an inch. Make a few more pleats and then turn the plate again. Keep going until the dumpling is almost closed. Twist the end at the top, and then using a small paring knife, cut off the twist at the very top.

8 Repeat to form all the dumplings and set them on a plate until ready to cook.

9 Bring a large pot of salted water to a boil. Add 1 tablespoon of olive oil to the pot (this will help prevent the dumplings from sticking together while cooking).

10 Boil the dumplings for 15 minutes.

11 Remove from the pot with a spider or slotted spoon. Top with lots of freshly ground black pepper and fresh dill.

Syrian Cheese Sambousek

Makes 4 dozen pastries

You would be hard pressed to find a Syrian home where sambousek aren't a regular part of the table. Sambousek are a traditional cheese pastry made with a simple crust, which are served for both everyday consumption, and holidays alike. Think of them as a Middle Eastern mini calzone or empanada; they are similar to Israeli-style bourekas, but the dough is different (and actually much easier to make).

I learned to make sambousek from my dear friend Miriam Golan, who makes them in large batches and freezes them. She puts them in her kids' lunches, brings a batch every time they go on a road trip, and always serves them for such holidays as Shavuot, when dairy is traditionally enjoyed.

What I have always found most interesting about Syrian sambousek in America is that they are most often made with Muenster, which is German in origin. It's a true expression of the evolution of Jewish cuisines in America: a classic Middle Eastern pastry, adapted in the United States, made with a German cheese because that was what was available and kosher. Many Syrian families also use a tortilla press to form the dough into perfectly flat rounds to fill for the pastry, another brilliant expression of how cuisines and culture adapt as they travel.

Regardless of the evolution of these delightful pastries, they are so buttery, delicious, and a perfect crowd-pleaser. They also freeze well and are a great finger food. You can delicately crimp the edges like an empanada, or channel your inner Syrian grandma and twist the edges into perfect pleats.

One final note about why this recipe is so fantastic: The dough does not need to be chilled ahead of time, so there is no heavy prepping if you are ready to create these homemade pastries. This recipe makes a large batch, 50 to 60 pastries.

If you want to freeze these pastries, shape them completely and then freeze them, unbaked, in a single layer on a baking sheet. Once they are frozen, transfer to a resealable plastic freezer bag. When ready to bake, brush with egg wash, top with sesame seeds, and bake for 25 to 30 minutes.

For the dough:

2 cups unbleached all-purpose flour

1 cup semolina flour

16 tablespoons (2 sticks) unsalted butter, at room temperature

½ cup warm water

¼ teaspoon kosher salt

1 Preheat the oven to 350°F.

2 **Make the dough:** Combine the flours, butter, and salt in a food processor fitted with the blade attachment. Pulse a few times, then add the warm water slowly until the dough comes together and forms a ball.

3 Wrap the dough in plastic wrap and set aside until ready to assemble the pastries. The dough does not need to be refrigerated.

recipe continues

For the filling:

1 pound Muenster, shredded

1 large egg, beaten

For assembly:

1 large egg, beaten

Sesame seeds

Black sesame seeds or nigella seeds (optional)

4 **Make the filling:** Gently combine the shredded cheese with the beaten egg in a medium bowl.

5 **To assemble:** Divide the dough into walnut-size balls. Press the balls into disks, using a tortilla press, a large pot and a piece of parchment paper, or a rolling pin.

6 Place 1 heaping teaspoon of cheese filling on a dough disk and fold the disk in half. Firmly pinch the ends closed and either crimp with a fork or press the edge of the dough between your thumb and forefinger, twisting the edge inward. Repeat to form the other pastries.

7 Brush with the beaten egg and top with sesame seeds and black sesame seeds (if using).

8 Bake for 20 to 25 minutes, until golden brown.

Syrian Cheese and Olive Bites

Makes 4 dozen pastries

These olive and cheese pastries are actually a variation on sambousek (page 135). It's the same dough, just shaped differently. So, if you make the sambousek dough, you could actually make half sambousek filled with cheese, and half these olive pastries. They are perfect for a finger food at a party.

For the dough:

1 cup unbleached all-purpose flour
½ cup semolina flour
8 tablespoons (1 stick) unsalted butter, at room temperature
⅛ teaspoon kosher salt
1 cup shredded Muenster
¼ cup warm water

For assembly:

Sesame seeds
Green olives with pimientos

1 Preheat the oven to 350°F.

2 **Make the dough:** Combine the flours, butter, salt, and cheese in a food processor fitted with the blade attachment. Pulse a few times, then add the warm water slowly until the dough comes together and forms a ball.

3 Roll tablespoon-size balls in the palm of your hand. Dip each ball into sesame seeds and place on a baking sheet lined with parchment paper.

4 Place an olive in the middle of each ball and gently press down.

5 Bake for 20 to 25 minutes, until slightly golden.

Classic Potato Knishes

Makes 2 dozen mini knishes

Potato knishes are ubiquitous with the Lower East Side of New York City, where knishes started to become popular from Ukrainian and Polish Jewish immigrants at the turn of the 20th century. Knishes were portable, cheap, filling, and delicious. In 1910, the first knish-specific bakery opened, and more followed suit. Later in the 20th century, Jewish delis and restaurants started serving them on their menu. Today, you can pick up a knish at almost any street corner or bodega in the city. Usually these are square, fried, and filled with savory potato filling.

The original knishes introduced by Jewish immigrants were round, likely to be filled with potato or kasha (buckwheat groats), a popular grain used in eastern Europe. Potato, kasha, and spinach knishes can still be found at Jewish delis around the country, but so can other varieties stuffed with everything from hot dogs and piled-high pastrami to even cheese and jalapeños.

I like making smaller knishes, which are great as party appetizers or even packed up for lunch.

For the dough:

2⅓ cups unbleached all-purpose flour, plus more for dusting

½ cup cold water

¼ cup vegetable or canola oil

1 large egg

½ teaspoon fine sea salt

For the filling:

1 russet potato, peeled and chopped

2 tablespoons olive oil or schmaltz

1 large onion, diced

Salt and freshly ground black pepper

To assemble:

1 large egg, beaten

Coarse sea salt (optional)

1 **Make the dough:** Place all the dough ingredients in a food processor. Pulse until the dough comes together. Transfer the dough to a lightly floured surface. Knead, using the palm of your hands, until the dough becomes smooth and elastic, about 3 minutes.

2 Wrap in plastic wrap and let it rest in the fridge for 1 hour.

3 **Make the filling:** Bring a pot of salted water to a boil and cook the potato for 7 to 10 minutes, until fork-tender. Drain and allow to cool slightly.

4 When the potato has cooled a few minutes, mash it.

5 Heat 1 tablespoon of the olive oil in a pan. Sauté the onion until translucent, 5 to 8 minutes. Add a pinch each of salt and pepper. Combine the onion and mashed potato with the remaining tablespoon of olive oil. Add a pinch more salt, if desired (remember—potatoes need a lot of seasoning).

6 Preheat the oven to 375°F.

7 After the dough has rested, divide it into two equal pieces and roll out each piece into a rectangle around 16 inches long and 8 inches wide. You want the dough to be around ¼ inch thick; the dough will keep bouncing back, so just keep rolling and know this is normal.

8 Shape the filling into a log along one long end of the dough. Roll up the dough until you form a log.

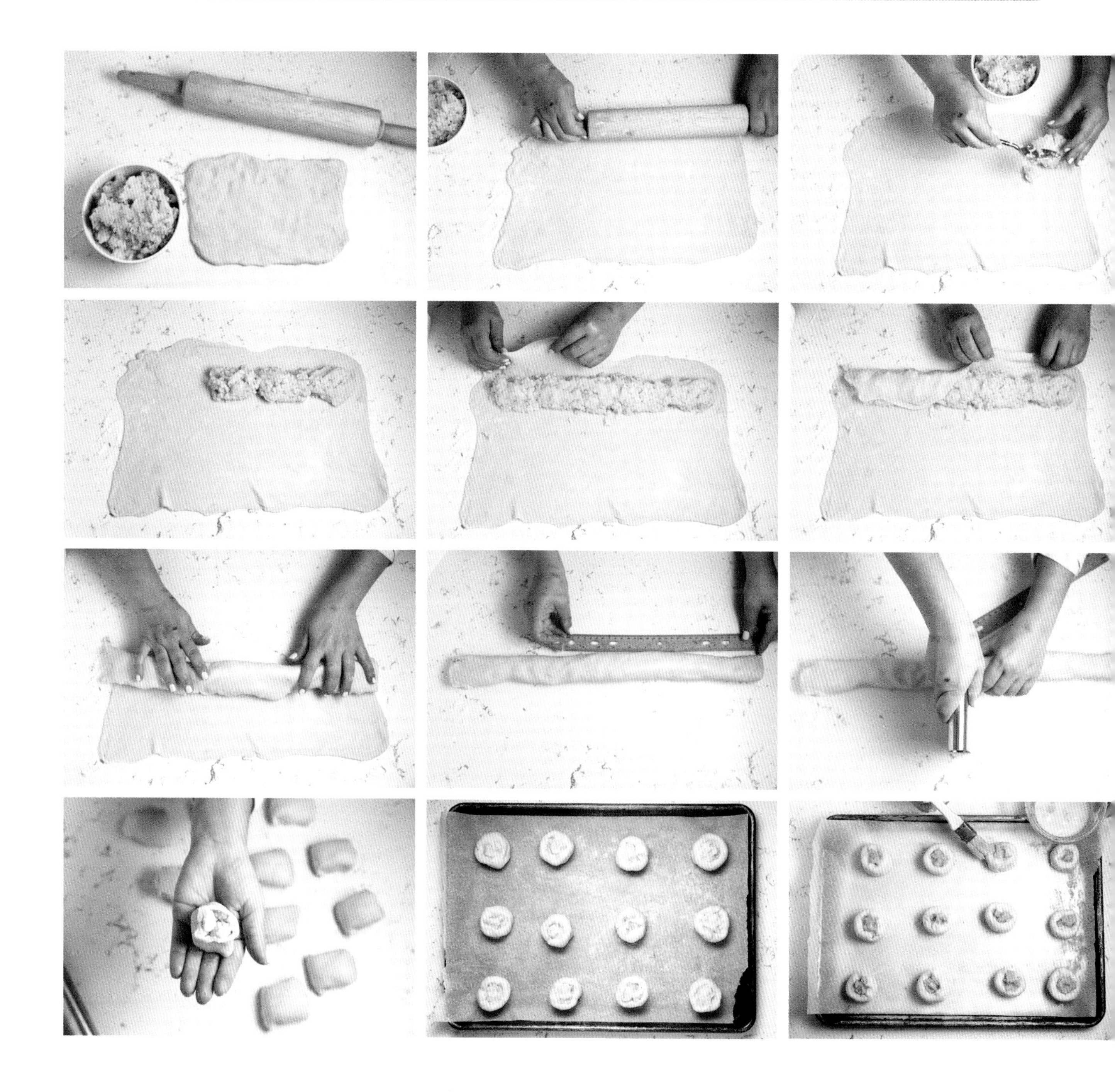

9 Cut each log into about eight pieces. Place the knishes on a baking sheet lined with parchment paper. Brush each knish with the beaten egg and top with coarse sea salt, if desired.

10 Bake for 20 to 25 minutes, until just golden.

Sweet Potato and Sage Butter Knishes

Makes 2 dozen mini knishes

Knishes are such a perfect finger food for parties or entertaining, and this sweet potato version is my own nod to autumn flavors. If you want to make this recipe nondairy, replace the butter with olive oil.

For the dough:

2⅓ cups unbleached all-purpose flour, plus more for dusting

½ cup cold water

¼ cup vegetable or canola oil

1 large egg

½ teaspoon fine sea salt

For the filling:

1 medium sweet potato, peeled and diced

½ medium russet potato, peeled and diced

4 tablespoons (½ stick) unsalted butter

Fresh sage leaves

Salt and freshly ground black pepper

For assembly:

1 large egg, beaten

Coarse sea salt (optional)

1 **Make the dough:** Place all the dough ingredients in a food processor. Pulse until the dough comes together. Transfer the dough to a lightly floured surface. Knead, using the palm of your hands, until the dough becomes smooth and elastic, about 3 minutes.

2 Wrap in plastic wrap and let it rest in the fridge for 1 hour.

3 **Make the filling:** Bring a pot of salted water to a boil and cook the sweet and russet potatoes for 7 to 10 minutes, until fork-tender. Drain and allow to cool slightly.

4 When the potatoes have cooled for a few minutes, mash in a bowl.

5 Heat the butter in a small saucepan over medium-low heat until melted. Add the sage leaves and allow to bubble slightly for 1 to 2 minutes. Do not let the butter burn.

6 Remove and discard the sage leaves. Add the melted sage butter to the mashed potatoes. Add salt and pepper to taste.

7 Preheat the oven to 375°F.

8 After the dough has rested, divide into two equal pieces and roll out each piece into a rectangle around 16 inches long and 8 inches wide. You want the dough to be around ¼ inch thick; the dough will keep bouncing back, so just keep rolling and know this is normal.

9 Shape the filling into a log along one long end of the dough. Roll up the dough until you form a log.

10 Cut each log into about eight pieces. Place the knishes on a baking sheet lined with parchment paper. Brush each knish with beaten egg and top with coarse sea salt, if desired.

11 Bake for 20 to 25 minutes, until just golden.

Everything Bagel Knishes

Makes 2 dozen mini knishes

These savory knishes get an extra creamy kick from cream cheese, and a nice crunch and saltiness from the everything bagel spice. You could serve these as a finger food or even for brunch.

For the dough:

2⅓ cups unbleached all-purpose flour, plus more for dusting

½ cup cold water

¼ cup vegetable or canola oil

1 large egg

½ teaspoon fine sea salt

For the filling:

1 russet potato, peeled and chopped

1 large onion, diced

2 ounces cream cheese or goat cheese

2 tablespoons everything bagel spice (recipe follows)

2 to 3 tablespoons olive oil or schmaltz

Salt and freshly ground black pepper

For assembly:

1 large egg, beaten

Everything bagel spice

1 **Make the dough:** Place all the dough ingredients in a food processor. Pulse until the dough comes together. Transfer the dough to a lightly floured surface. Knead, using the palm of your hands, until the dough becomes smooth and elastic, about 3 minutes.

2 Wrap in plastic wrap and let it rest in the fridge for 1 hour.

3 **Make the filling:** Bring a pot of salted water to a boil and cook the potato for 7 to 10 minutes, until fork-tender. Drain and allow to cool slightly.

4 When the potato has cooled a few minutes, mash.

5 Heat 1 to 2 tablespoons of the olive oil in a pan over medium heat. Sauté the onion until translucent, 5 to 8 minutes. Add a pinch each of salt and pepper.

6 Combine the onion, mashed potato, remaining tablespoon of olive oil, cream cheese, and 2 tablespoons everything bagel spice

7 Preheat the oven to 375°F.

8 After the dough has rested, divide into two equal pieces and roll out each piece into a rectangle around 16 inches long and 8 inches wide. You want the dough to be around ¼ inch thick; the dough will keep bouncing back, so just keep rolling and know this is normal.

9 Shape the filling into a log along one long end of the dough. Roll up the dough until you form a log.

10 Cut each log into about eight pieces. Place the knishes on a baking sheet lined with parchment paper. Brush each knish with the beaten egg and top with additional everything bagel spice.

11 Bake for 20 to 25 minutes, until just golden.

Make Your Own Everything Bagel Spice

You can buy everything bagel spice at almost every major supermarket these days, but it's also fun to make your own. Combine 2 tablespoons of sesame seeds, 2 tablespoons of poppy seeds, 2 tablespoons of dried minced garlic, and 2 tablespoons of dried minced onion. You can add 1½ teaspoons of red pepper flakes if you like things spicy.

CHAPTER 8

Latkes

Let's talk about latkes.

Latkes are one of the most recognizable and beloved eastern European Jewish foods. Traditionally served for Hanukkah, they are significant not because of the latke ingredients but because they are fried in oil, representative of the miracle when the oil that lasted eight nights saved the Jewish people in Israel. Every Jewish cuisine has its own unique dish served for Hanukkah, from Moroccan *sfenj* to Persian *zoulbia* to sweet Italian fritters.

Latkes (and other fritters) are a relatively easy food to make. They also come in lots of varieties and can be adapted for tastes, diets, and which ingredients you have around. I've made latkes with plantains, broccoli stems, sweet potatoes, and lots of other veggies. Use these recipes as a jumping-off point, and have fun experimenting.

Here are a few tips for making perfect latkes every time:

- If using potatoes, don't wring out all that extra liquid. You want to save the starchy liquid that forms at the bottom and add it back. The starch will actually make the latkes crispier on the outside and help them bind together.
- Fry a test latke first to check for seasoning. If it seems right, proceed ahead. If not, adjust the seasoning to taste.
- When the latkes come out of the pan, immediately sprinkle them with a touch more salt, which will adhere to the hot oil and really enhance the flavor.
- Do not place your freshly fried latkes on top of paper towels. Rather, let them cool on wire racks, which will prevent them from getting soggy.
- As the latkes are frying, you will want to add more oil to the pan, as it will be absorbed and reduce as the latkes are fried. Also try to remove any bits of burnt potato or vegetable pieces that float in the oil. If the oil becomes too dark, discard and start with fresh oil.
- To reheat latkes, place them on wire racks (not directly on the oven racks) in a preheated 300°F oven and heat until warmed through.
- Potato and other root vegetable latkes do freeze well and can be reheated to serve. After you fry the latkes and they have cooled, freeze between pieces of parchment paper and place in a resealable plastic freezer bag.

CLASSIC Potato Latkes

Makes 16 to 24 latkes

I love making different types of latkes, but there is nothing quite like the perfect, freshly fried potato latke topped with applesauce and sour cream. My other favorite way to serve potato latkes is with crème fraîche, smoked salmon, or if you're feeling extra fancy, some caviar.

4 russet potatoes, peeled
1 large onion
2 large eggs
¼ cup unbleached all-purpose flour or matzah meal
2 teaspoons fine sea salt, plus more for sprinkling
½ teaspoon freshly ground black pepper
Vegetable oil for frying

1 Using a food processor or a box grater, shred the potatoes and onion.

2 Combine the potatoes, onion, eggs, flour, salt, and pepper in a large bowl and allow to sit for 5 minutes.

3 Once the mixture has sat for 5 minutes, liquid will have accumulated in the bowl. You want to drain off most of this liquid, though not all of it. As you pour off the liquid, some starch will have settled at the bottom of the bowl. Add that starchy bit back to your potato mixture, as this starch will help bind the latkes, making them crispy on the outside and creamy on the inside.

4 Heat oil in a large skillet over medium-high heat.

5 Fry the latkes in batches of three or four until golden and crispy on each side, then place on a wire rack on top of a baking sheet to cool.

6 Sprinkle with salt when they are done frying.

7 Serve with applesauce, sour cream, or other fun toppings.

recipe continues

SERVE WITH

Pulled Brisket

Serves 6 to 8

Although brisket is not a traditional food for Hanukkah, many American Jewish families serve it then. Indeed, they use every celebratory occasion to present such beloved family dishes as brisket and kugel. Instead of serving a big sliced brisket alongside latkes, I like to top those crispy potato latkes with rich, pulled brisket. The contrasting textures and flavors all play off one another nicely and guests will love this combination.

One 3- to 4-pound brisket
Salt and freshly ground black pepper
2 tablespoons olive oil
2 onions, diced
4 or 5 carrots, peeled and diced
2 garlic cloves, minced
2 teaspoons onion salt or other preferred seasoning
¼ cup ketchup
2 cups sweet red wine, such as Manischewitz, or cola or root beer
1 cup chicken, vegetable, or beef stock, or water
1 tablespoon balsamic vinegar

1 Remove any excess moisture from the brisket with a paper towel. Season all over with salt and pepper.

2 Heat 1 to 2 tablespoons of the olive oil in a large Dutch oven over medium-high heat.

3 Sear the brisket on both sides until a nice crust forms. Remove from the pan and set aside.

4 Lower the heat to medium. Add the onions and carrots to the pan and sauté for 10 to 12 minutes, scraping up any brown bits from the bottom of the pan. Add the garlic and cook for another 2 to 3 minutes.

5 Add the onion salt, ketchup, red wine, and stock or water. Place the brisket back in the pan.

6 Lower the heat to low and cook for 3 to 4 hours, checking a few times. If the liquid has reduced too much, add more stock and/or wine. Season with salt and pepper to taste.

7 During the last 20 minutes of cooking, add the balsamic vinegar.

8 Remove the brisket from the sauce and let it cool completely. Once the brisket is cool enough to handle (or even better, has been refrigerated), pull apart, using two forks.

9 **Optional step:** While the brisket cools, use a food processor or handheld immersion blender to pulse the sauce until smooth. The carrots will make the sauce creamy and slightly sweet. Add the sauce to the pulled brisket.

SERVE WITH

Easiest Applesauce Ever

Makes 3 cups

4 apples
¾ cup water

1 Peel, core, and dice the apples. Place in a medium pot and add the water. Bring to a boil, then lower the heat to medium-low. Cook until the apples are soft.

2 Transfer to a food processor and pulse until they reach your desired consistency.

Beet and Carrot Latkes

Makes 16 to 24 latkes

While potato latkes are my classic favorite, these brightly hued beet and carrot latkes are a close second. They have a surprising sweet and savory flavor, and I love making them to serve alongside my classic potato latkes every year.

- 2 medium beets, peeled
- 1 large carrot, peeled
- 1 medium russet potato, peeled
- 2 large eggs
- 3 tablespoons all-purpose flour
- 1 teaspoon fresh thyme, plus more for garnish
- 1 to 2 teaspoons fine sea salt, plus more for sprinkling
- Vegetable oil for frying

1 Cut the beets and carrot in half. In three or four batches, run the beets, carrot, and potatoes through a food processor to coarsely grate. Alternatively, grate coarsely by hand.

2 Place the grated vegetables in a large bowl. Add the eggs, flour, thyme, and salt.

3 Heat around ¼ cup of vegetable oil in a large sauté pan over medium-high heat. Form bite-size mounds of the vegetable mixture, taking care not to squeeze too much liquid out of the mixture. Fry until browned and crispy on each side, then place on a wire rack on top of a baking sheet to cool. Immediately sprinkle with a pinch of salt.

4 Serve warm with applesauce, sour cream, and some additional fresh thyme for garnish.

Herb Zucchini Potato Latkes

Makes 16 to 24 latkes

In Persian, Syrian, and other Middle Eastern Jewish communities, fresh herbs are used generously to season rice dishes, frittatas, and stews. These zucchini and potato latkes get an extra herbaceous infusion with a combination of parsley, dill, and cilantro, but you could also try other combinations of fresh herbs, such as mint or chives. For extra brightness, try adding a little squeeze of lemon juice.

2 medium zucchini, peeled
1 medium russet potato, peeled
1 small onion
2 large eggs
2 to 3 tablespoons all-purpose flour
1 tablespoon chopped fresh parsley
1 tablespoon chopped fresh dill
1 tablespoon chopped fresh cilantro
1 teaspoon salt, plus more for sprinkling
¼ teaspoon freshly ground black pepper
Wedges of lemon (optional)
Vegetable oil for frying

1 Cut the zucchini, potato, and onion in half. In three or four batches, run the vegetables through a food processor to coarsely grate. Alternatively, grate coarsely by hand.

2 Transfer the mixture to a large bowl. Add the eggs, flour, parsley, dill, cilantro, salt, and pepper.

3 Heat around ¼ cup of vegetable oil in a large sauté pan over medium-high heat. Form bite-size mounds of the mixture, taking care not to squeeze too much liquid out of the mixture. Fry until golden brown on each side, then place on a wire rack on top of a baking sheet to cool. Immediately sprinkle with a pinch of salt.

4 Serve warm with sour cream or crème fraîche and a squeeze of lemon juice, if desired.

Beet-Cured Gravlax

Serves 4 to 6

One of my favorite ways to serve potato latkes is with smoked salmon. For Hanukkah and Passover, I like to take the extra step to make my own gravlax for serving with potato latkes, which I think is one of the most perfect flavor pairings. The salty, crunchy potato latkes contrast with the cool, briny gravlax and the combination is heavenly.

Making your own gravlax seems fancy and complicated, but is actually a very simple task. In this version, grated raw beets add a beautiful hue to the salmon, but you could leave them off if you don't like beets.

1 cup sugar
½ cup kosher salt
Freshly ground black pepper
2 small beets, peeled and grated
1 large bunch dill
Zest of 1 lemon
1 pound fresh salmon filet

1 Combine the sugar, salt, pepper, beets, dill, and lemon zest in a bowl.

2 Lay a piece of plastic wrap on a baking sheet or a large platter. Spread a layer of the mixture on the plastic wrap, just larger than the piece of salmon.

3 Place the salmon, skin side down, on top of the mixture. Spread the remaining mixture on top of the salmon.

4 Wrap the salmon tightly in plastic wrap and place on a platter or plate in the fridge for 3 to 5 days.

5 When you are ready to serve, remove from the fridge and drain the liquid. Remove and discard the beet mixture and rinse the salmon in cold water. Pat dry with a paper towel.

6 Slice into thin pieces, discarding the skin, and serve.

Cheese Latkes

Serves 4 to 6

Although potato latkes are probably the most widely known version in the United States, they are actually far from the original that, for centuries, was made with soft cheese, not potatoes. Potatoes were not introduced to Europe until after the 16th century. Eventually potatoes became much cheaper and more widely available for eastern European Jews, and cheese latkes fell out of fashion.

My children absolutely love cheese pancakes. The taste of these will remind you of the inside of a blintz, and who doesn't love blintzes? We serve cheese latkes with some good jam or even maple syrup sometimes. I know many families love to make them for Passover as well, which just requires you to substitute matzah meal for the flour.

1 cup cottage cheese
1 cup farmer cheese
1 cup milk
2 large eggs
1 teaspoon vanilla extract or lemon zest
2 tablespoons sugar
1 cup all-purpose flour or matzah meal
¼ teaspoon salt
1 teaspoon baking powder
Vegetable oil for frying
1 teaspoon unsalted butter for frying

1 Combine the cheeses, milk, eggs, and vanilla or lemon zest in a medium bowl.

2 In a separate bowl, whisk together the flour, sugar, salt, and baking powder.

3 Add the flour mixture to the cheese mixture.

4 Heat a few tablespoons of vegetable oil and the butter in a large sauté pan over medium heat.

5 Scoop around ¼ cup of the batter onto the pan to form a cheese latke. Fry until golden on each side, 2 to 3 minutes. The latke will be quite thin; do not be alarmed. Repeat with the remaining batter.

6 Serve with powdered sugar, cinnamon sugar, sour cream, or jam.

Smoked Salmon Latkes Eggs Benedict

Serves 4

When I am having a small group for brunch, this is my favorite dish to make. It's also perfect to make during Passover, when satisfying breakfasts can sometimes be a challenge. You could make homemade gravlax for this, but it's just as good with some good-quality, store-bought smoked salmon. Whole Foods typically has a great selection, and many stores around the country carry Acme fish products, which are excellent.

If smoked fish isn't your thing, you could replace it with sautéed spinach, turkey bacon, or goat cheese and a nice slice of tomato.

This recipe will serve approximately four adults, but you can adjust it depending on the number of people you are feeding.

2 tablespoons white distilled vinegar
Salt
8 large eggs
Good-quality smoked salmon or gravlax
8 Classic Potato Latkes (page 148), warmed
Fresh dill (optional)

1 Make your poached eggs: Fill a medium saucepan three-quarters of the way full with water. Bring to a simmer. Add the vinegar and a pinch of salt.

2 Using a spoon, gently swirl the water. Crack an egg into a small bowl and slowly pour into the middle of the water, taking care not to break the yolk. Set a timer for 3 minutes. After 3 minutes, remove the egg with a slotted spoon and place on a paper towel or clean tea towel. Repeat, working one at a time, to cook each of the remaining eggs.

3 Place a slice of smoked salmon on top of each warmed latke. Place a poached egg on top of the smoked salmon and a sprig of dill on top of each, if desired.

4 Serve while warm.

Summer Corn Zucchini Latkes

Makes 10 to 12 latkes

These corn and zucchini latkes are perfect during the summer for a fun weeknight dinner, but of course you could make them all year and even use about a cup of frozen corn in a pinch. I like to serve these with some store-bought tzatziki or Greek yogurt.

1 medium zucchini, ends trimmed
½ teaspoon salt, plus more for sprinkling
1 large russet potato
Kernels from 2 ears of fresh corn
2 large eggs
3 to 4 tablespoons whole wheat flour, unbleached all-purpose flour, or matzah meal
¼ teaspoon freshly ground black pepper
Vegetable oil for frying

1 Coarsely grate the zucchini and place in a medium bowl with ¼ teaspoon of the salt. Allow to sit for 20 minutes. After 20 minutes, place the shredded zucchini in a clean kitchen towel and wring out any excess water.

2 Shred the raw potato in a food processor or using a grater.

3 Place the shredded potato, zucchini, corn kernels, eggs, flour, pepper, and remaining ¼ teaspoon of salt in a large bowl. Mix until combined.

4 Heat 2 to 3 tablespoons of vegetable oil in a large sauté pan over medium-high heat.

5 Form the mixture into patties, using approximately ⅓ cup per patty.

6 Cook until golden and crispy on first side, 3 to 4 minutes. Flip and cook for another 2 to 3 minutes.

7 Place on a wire baking rack and add a pinch of salt immediately.

Sephardic Leek Patties

Serves 4 to 6

Leeks feature prominently in Sephardic cooking (Sephardim are Jews of Spanish/Iberian descent) and are even considered a symbolic food for the Jewish New Year. Leek fritters or patties can be made in lots of different ways; the ingredients and ratios vary from tradition to tradition and family to family.

I learned to make these from my friend and colleague Sylvia Fallas. Instead of mashing her potato as I do, she grates it; you could try it both ways to see which you prefer. You could also add chopped fresh herbs to the mixture, or even some feta. As Sylvia taught me, leek patties, or *edje* in the Syrian tradition, are endlessly adaptable.

4 large leeks (around 2 pounds)

1 russet potato (around 1 pound), peeled and cut into chunks

4 large eggs

½ cup bread crumbs or matzah meal

1 teaspoon fine sea salt, plus more for sprinkling

Vegetable oil for frying

Lemon wedges and fresh herbs for serving (optional)

1 Trim the root and dark green parts of the leeks. Split down the middle and rinse under cold water. Cut into rings around ½ inch long and soak in a large bowl of cool water for 5 minutes.

2 Do not pour out the water; rather, scoop the leeks from the water with your hands or a spider and transfer to clean dish towels. Blot to remove any excess water.

3 Meanwhile, bring a small saucepan of salted water to a boil. Cook the potato for 7 to 10 minutes, or until fork-tender. Drain and allow to cool slightly.

4 Transfer the potato to a large bowl and mash. Add the eggs, bread crumbs, salt, and leeks and combine.

5 Heat around ¼ cup of vegetable oil in a large sauté pan over medium-high heat. Using a tablespoon to form each pancake, gently place it in the oil. Flatten with the bottom of a spatula. Cook for 3 to 4 minutes on each side, until golden brown.

6 Place on a wire rack on top of a baking sheet to cool. Immediately sprinkle with a pinch of salt. Serve with lemon wedges and fresh herbs, if desired.

CHAPTER 9

Sweets

Let's talk about sweets.

This book is all about comfort food and as a baker with a serious sweet tooth, it's just not a meal, holiday, or an afternoon coffee break without a sweet bite. There are so many fantastic Jewish cookies, cakes, and sweets spanning diverse traditions, but the three things that influenced the sweets on the following pages were desserts that were nostalgic for me: black-and-white cookies that transport me back to the bakery in Yonkers with my grandmother, holding her hand and waiting in anticipation for my special treat; holidays and parties with platters of rainbow cookies that my mom would buy, and my brother and I would wait impatiently to get our hands on; and trips to the *shuk* (Machane Yehuda market) in Jerusalem, licking sticky rugelach filling from my fingers while plastic bags full of gifts and treats hung from every part of my body.

Many of the treats in this chapter may seem like daunting tasks to re-create at home, but that's what makes them feel special and exciting: to tackle homemade black-and-white cookies or rainbow cookies, which are readily available at New York–style bakeries in America, but are even more satisfying when homemade.

Other traditional treats, like macaroons and mandel bread, gain new life with homemade versions that have unexpected flavors and toppings. Some desserts, such as chocolate hazelnut swirl cookies, are meant for everyday entertaining or enjoyment; others are meant just a few times during the year for celebrations or holidays.

Sweets and memories just go hand in hand, and for every person, those memories are slightly different. This selection of cookies and desserts are particularly sentimental to me, and are meant to bring joy to every day and holidays alike. I also hope these recipes provide space for adding your own flavors and interpretation, and most important, for inspiring sweet memories.

Israeli Chocolate Hazelnut Swirl Cookies

Makes 2 dozen cookies

These "swirl" cookies may look similar to rugelach, a classic eastern European cookie that is also shaped like a swirl, but the dough—and its origin—is different. Sometimes called Israeli café cookies, they are a home treat that many Israeli bakers make weekly.

These sweets are the perfect accompaniment to an afternoon cup of tea or coffee. They are also the perfect treat to throw together at the last minute for guests because the dough only needs to chill for 20 minutes, and the shaping is simple, which makes the task of whipping these up almost easier than opening a box of brownie mix.

3 cups unbleached all-purpose flour
2½ teaspoons baking powder
¼ teaspoon salt
14 tablespoons (1½ sticks + 2 tablespoons) unsalted butter, at room temperature
¼ cup sugar
1 cup full-fat sour cream
1 cup chocolate hazelnut spread, such as Nutella, for spreading
Powdered sugar for sprinkling

1 Combine the flour, baking powder, and salt in a medium bowl.

2 Using a handheld mixer and a separate medium bowl or a stand mixer fitted with the paddle attachment, beat together the butter and sugar. Add the sour cream and beat until combined.

3 Add the sour cream mixture to the flour mixture and beat until just combined.

4 Wrap in plastic wrap and place in the fridge to chill for 20 minutes.

5 Preheat the oven to 375°F. Unwrap the dough and divide into two equal pieces. (Use a food scale for precision if you have one.)

6 Roll each piece of dough into a rectangle around 8 by 14 inches. Spread the chocolate hazelnut spread evenly across one dough rectangle.

7 Working from the longer end, firmly roll up the dough (not loosely as you might for cinnamon rolls or babka). As you roll up the dough, create more of a square-shaped log, not perfectly round. Repeat with the other piece of dough.

8 Place each roll on a baking sheet lined with parchment paper.

9 Using a sharp knife, cut indentations spaced 1 inch apart (not cutting all the way through the cookies, just through the top). This step will make it easier after the rolls are baked to cut them into pieces.

10 Bake for 26 to 28 minutes, until slightly golden. You can rotate the baking sheets halfway through baking, for more even baking.

11 Remove from the oven and let cool slightly. Sprinkle all over with powdered sugar. Slice through each slit to separate into cookies.

Israeli Date & Walnut Swirl Cookies

Makes 2 dozen cookies

Some say these cookies, filled with date and walnuts, are a cousin to traditional Middle Eastern *ma'moul*, a shaped date cookie made with semolina flour.

Buying a can of premade date paste makes the task of baking these cookies very simple. Kosher markets or even Whole Foods will have prepared date paste from several different brands. A thick fig jam could also work if dates are too strong a flavor.

3 cups unbleached all-purpose flour
2½ teaspoons baking powder
¼ teaspoon salt
14 tablespoons (1½ sticks + 2 tablespoons) unsalted butter, at room temperature
¼ cup sugar
1 cup full-fat sour cream
1 cup date paste
¾ cup chopped walnuts

1 Combine the flour, baking powder, and salt in a medium bowl.

2 Using a handheld mixer and a separate medium bowl or a stand mixer fitted with the paddle attachment, beat together the butter and sugar. Add the sour cream and beat until combined.

3 Add the flour mixture to the sour cream mixture and beat until just combined.

4 Wrap in plastic wrap and place in the fridge to chill for 20 minutes.

5 Preheat the oven to 375°F and line two baking sheets with parchment paper.

6 Unwrap the dough and divide into two equal pieces. (Use a food scale for precision if you have one.)

7 Roll each piece of dough into a rectangle around 8 by 14 inches.

8 Spread the date paste evenly across one dough rectangle.

9 Working from the longer end, firmly roll up the dough (not loosely as you might for cinnamon rolls or babka). As you roll up the dough, create more of a square-shaped log, not perfectly round. Repeat with the other piece of dough.

10 Place each roll on a prepared baking sheet.

11 Using a sharp knife, cut indentations spaced 1 inch apart (not cutting all the way through the cookies, just through the top). This step will make it easier after the rolls are baked to cut them into pieces.

12 Bake for 26 to 28 minutes, until slightly golden. You can rotate the baking sheets halfway through baking.

13 Remove from the oven and allow to cool slightly. Sprinkle all over with powdered sugar. Then, slice all the way through each slit to separate into cookies.

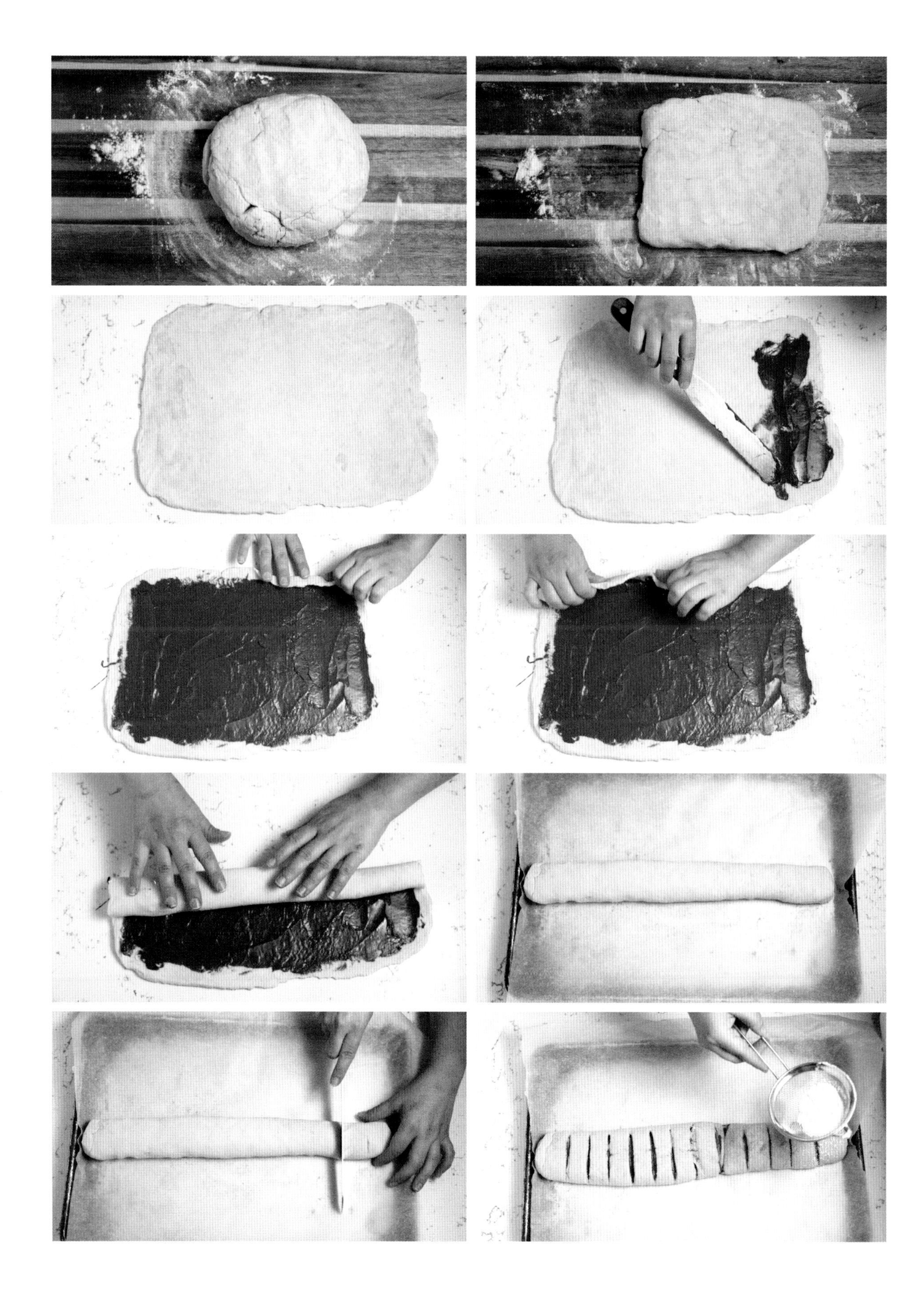

Black & White Cookies

Makes 12 to 18 cookies

If you grew up in the New York area, black-and-white cookies are everywhere: at the supermarket, at the bagel shop, and bakeries, too. There are two competing theories explaining their origins. Some say that black-and-white cookies were invented at Glaser's Bakery, which had been located in Manhattan's Upper East Side neighborhood. Others claim that Utica, New York's "half-moon cookies" were the original black-and-whites. Regardless, these cookie-cakes are believed to be German or Dutch in origin, and are synonymous with New York City.

Of course, I cannot talk about black-and-whites without mentioning the infamous *Seinfeld* episode, "look to the cookie!" If you don't know this reference, go to YouTube immediately, search for the episode, and enjoy. While you're at it, binge watch the entire show.

You could make extra-large cookies with this recipe, which will yield fewer cookies. My preference is to make smaller cookies, using a 2-inch cookie scoop. Because eating more cookies is just more fun. Once you make your own, you'll never go back to the store-bought variety again.

For the cookies:

1¼ cups unbleached all-purpose flour

½ teaspoon baking soda

⅛ teaspoon baking powder

½ teaspoon salt

⅓ cup buttermilk, or ⅓ cup whole milk + 1 teaspoon fresh lemon juice (let sit for 5 minutes)

½ teaspoon vanilla extract

Zest of 1 lemon (about 2 teaspoons)

5 tablespoons unsalted butter, at room temperature

½ cup granulated sugar

1 large egg

For the icing:

1 tablespoon light corn syrup

1 teaspoon vanilla extract

¼ cup + 2 teaspoons whole milk

2 cups (260 g) powdered sugar, sifted

3 tablespoons Dutch-processed cocoa powder

1 **Make the cookies:** Preheat the oven to 350°F. Line two baking sheets with parchment paper or silicone baking mats.

2 Whisk together the flour, baking soda, baking powder, and salt in a medium bowl.

3 Stir together the buttermilk, vanilla, and lemon zest in a measuring cup or small bowl.

4 Using a handheld mixer and a large bowl or a stand mixer fitted with the whisk attachment, beat together the butter and granulated sugar, until pale and fluffy, about 3 minutes. Add the egg and mix again until combined.

5 Alternate adding the flour mixture and the buttermilk mixture to the butter mixture, mixing on a low speed, until the batter is well combined and smooth.

6 Using a 2-inch cookie scoop or a heaping/rounded tablespoon, place mounds of batter about 2 inches apart on the prepared baking sheets. Dipping your pointer finger in water, smooth the circumference of each cookie to ensure it is round.

7 Bake 10 for 12 minutes, until the tops are puffed and slightly golden (check the underside of one of the cookies at around 8 minutes).

8 Remove the cookies from the baking sheets and place on a rack to cool for about 1 hour before icing.

recipe continues

9 **Make the icing:** Mix together the corn syrup, vanilla, and ¼ cup of the milk in a small bowl until smooth. Add the sifted powdered sugar and whisk until smooth. Transfer half of the icing to another bowl and stir in the cocoa powder and remaining 2 teaspoons of milk (consistency of both icings should be about the same; adjust the milk as needed). (See Note for another way to color the icing.)

10 **To ice the cookies:** Turn the cookies upside down. Always start with the white icing. Use a spoon or knife to "push" icing over half of each cookie. Let set and then repeat to add the chocolate icing next to the white icing, to form two joined, contrasting semicircles of icing. Alternatively, place a bowl scraper or parchment paper over half of each cookie and spread the uncovered half with white icing, using a small offset spatula. Allow to set 10 for 15 minutes. When the icing has set, frost the bare half of the cookies with the chocolate icing. Allow to set for another 10 to 15 minutes until serving.

11 Store in an airtight container for 2 to 3 days.

Note: **Alternatively, after mixing the white icing, use it to ice each entire upside-down cookie instead of only half of each cookie, and while the white icing is starting to set, mix the cocoa powder and 2 teaspoons of milk into the bowl of leftover white icing (you'll have lots) to make the chocolate icing. Apply the chocolate icing to one side of the white icing atop each cookie, to form two joined, contrasting semicircles of icing.**

Coconut Macaroons

Makes 1 dozen macaroons

Macaroons get a really bad reputation. After all, it's impossible to find a kosher aisle of the supermarket without those canisters of dry, sawdustlike cookies. Coconut macaroons are incredibly simple to make, come together quickly, and are a really satisfying sweet during Passover, or anytime.

For the cookies:

2 large egg whites
2 cups sweetened shredded coconut
½ cup chopped almonds
⅓ cup sugar
1 teaspoon vanilla extract
¼ teaspoon salt

For the chocolate drizzle:

½ cup semisweet or dark chocolate chips
½ teaspoon vegetable or coconut oil

1 **Make the cookies:** Preheat the oven to 350°F. Line a baking sheet with parchment paper.

2 Combine the egg whites, coconut, and almonds in a large bowl. Add the sugar, vanilla, and salt and stir to combine. Using a cookie scoop, portion out the batter around 2 inches apart onto the prepared baking sheet.

3 Bake until the cookies are set and the edges begin to crisp, around 15 minutes.

4 Remove from the oven and allow to cool completely.

5 **Make the drizzle:** In a microwave-safe bowl, combine the chocolate chips and oil. Microwave in 30-second intervals, stirring gently in between, until the chocolate is completely melted.

6 Drizzle the melted chocolate over the cookies, or dip the bottom of the cookies into the melted chocolate. Place on parchment paper for the drizzle to harden completely before serving.

Chocolate Chip Macaroons

Makes 1 dozen macaroons

A simple addition of mini chocolate chips takes coconut macaroons to the next level. Dip or drizzle your macaroons to make them extra fancy. These are anything but your supermarket macaroons.

For the cookies:
2 large egg whites
2 cups sweetened shredded coconut
½ cup chopped almonds
3 tablespoons mini chocolate chips
⅓ cup sugar
1 teaspoon vanilla extract
¼ teaspoon salt

For the chocolate drizzle:
½ cup semisweet or dark chocolate chips
½ teaspoon vegetable or coconut oil

1 **Make the cookies:** Preheat the oven to 350°F. Line a baking sheet with parchment paper.

2 Combine the egg whites, coconut, and almonds in a large bowl. Add the sugar, vanilla, and salt and stir to combine. Using a cookie scoop, portion out the batter around 2 inches apart onto the prepared baking sheet.

3 Bake until the cookies are set and the edges begin to crisp, around 15 minutes.

4 Remove from the oven and allow to cool completely.

5 **Make the drizzle:** In a microwave-safe bowl, combine the chocolate chips and oil. Microwave in 30-second intervals, stirring gently in between, until the chocolate is completely melted.

6 Drizzle the melted chocolate over the cookies, or dip the bottom of the cookies into the melted chocolate. Place on parchment paper for the drizzle to harden completely before serving.

Funfetti Coconut Macaroons

Makes 1 dozen macaroons

These brightly colored macaroons are sure to make anyone smile. There are definitely brands of kosher-for-Passover sprinkles available, including Lieber's and Oh! Nuts, which you can order online.

For the cookies:

2 large egg whites

2 cups sweetened shredded coconut

½ cup chopped almonds

⅓ cup sugar

1 teaspoon vanilla extract

¼ teaspoon salt

3 tablespoons multicolored sprinkles, plus more for garnish (optional)

For the chocolate drizzle:

½ cup good-quality white chocolate chips or bar chopped into pieces

½ teaspoon vegetable or coconut oil

1 **Make the cookies:** Preheat the oven to 350°F. Line a baking sheet with parchment paper.

2 Combine the egg whites, coconut, and almonds in a large bowl. Add the sugar, vanilla, salt, and sprinkles and mix to combine. Using a cookie scoop, portion out the batter around 2 inches apart onto the prepared baking sheet.

3 Bake until the cookies are set and the edges begin to crisp, around 15 minutes.

4 Remove from the oven and allow to cool completely.

5 **Make the drizzle:** In a microwave-safe bowl, combine the chocolate chips and oil. Microwave in 30-second intervals, stirring gently in between, until the chocolate is completely melted.

6 Drizzle the melted chocolate over the cookies and top with additional sprinkles, if desired. Place on parchment paper and allow the drizzle to harden completely before serving.

Peanut Butter Chocolate Coconut Macaroons

Makes 2 dozen macaroons

If a candy bar and a coconut macaroon had a love child, this sweet confection would be the result. You can replace the peanut butter with any nut butter you prefer. If you want to make these treats a tad less sweet, swap out the sweetened coconut for unsweetened. This recipe doubles perfectly to feed a larger crowd.

For the cookies:

2¾ cups sweetened shredded coconut
¼ cup coconut flour or almond flour
¼ teaspoon fine sea salt
7 ounces condensed milk
1 large egg
1 teaspoon vanilla extract
¾ cup creamy peanut butter
Cooking spray

For the topping:

½ cup semisweet or dark chocolate chips
½ teaspoon vegetable or coconut oil
Chopped salted peanuts (optional)
Coarse sea salt (optional)

1 **Make the cookies:** Preheat the oven to 350°F. Line a large baking sheet with parchment paper or a silicone baking mat.

2 Combine the shredded coconut, flour, and fine sea salt in a large bowl. In a separate bowl, combine the condensed milk, egg, vanilla, and peanut butter.

3 Add the peanut butter mixture to the coconut mixture and mix until combined.

4 Spray the inside of a 1½- or 2-inch cookie scoop with cooking spray. Scoop the batter and space the mounds around 1 inch apart on the prepared baking sheet.

5 Bake for 12 to 14 minutes, until the edges just begin to brown slightly.

6 Remove from the oven and allow to cool completely.

7 **Make the topping:** In a microwave-safe bowl, combine the chocolate chips and oil. Microwave in 30-second intervals, stirring gently in between, until the chocolate is completely melted.

8 Drizzle the melted chocolate over cookies. Top with chopped peanuts or coarse sea salt, if desired. Allow the chocolate to harden before serving.

Israeli-Style Yeasted Rugelach Two Ways

Makes 24 to 30 cookies

Rugelach are a Jewish sweet that diverged as they traveled from Europe to America, and to Israel. The American version got a cream cheese upgrade, and they transformed into a slightly easier cookie that could be made in less time. The Israeli version kept the yeasted dough, but also transformed into a very European-style confection. The recipe does take a little more finesse, but the result is sublime: tender, sweet, and just gooey enough.

This recipe allows you to pick the filling of your choice: chocolate or cinnamon.

For the dough:

3 teaspoons active dry yeast
1 cup milk, at room temperature
1 large egg
¼ cup granulated sugar
5 tablespoons unsalted butter, melted
4 cups unbleached all-purpose flour
¼ teaspoon salt
Cooking spray for the bowl

For the chocolate filling:

12 tablespoons (1½ sticks) unsalted butter, at room temperature
⅓ cup unsweetened cocoa powder
½ cup powdered sugar
½ teaspoon ground cinnamon
¼ teaspoon fine sea salt

For the cinnamon filling:

12 tablespoons (1½ sticks) unsalted butter, at room temperature
1½ cups granulated sugar
2 tablespoons all-purpose flour
2 tablespoons ground cinnamon
¼ teaspoon salt

For the syrup:

½ cup granulated sugar
½ cup water
1 teaspoon vanilla extract (optional)

1 Line a baking sheet with parchment paper or a silicone baking mat. Set aside until ready to use.

2 **Make the dough:** Combine the yeast, milk, egg, granulated sugar, melted butter, flour, and salt in a stand mixer fitted with the hook attachment. Mix on medium-high speed for 3 to 5 minutes, until the dough is smooth and easily pulls away from the side of the bowl.

3 Place in a bowl greased with cooking spray and cover with plastic wrap. Allow to rise in a warm place for 1 hour.

4 **Prepare your filling of choice:** Combine all the filling ingredients in a medium bowl.

5 **Assemble the rugelach:** Divide dough into two equal pieces. (If you aren't good at estimating, which I am not, use a digital food scale to weigh out the dough and then divide in half.)

6 Roll each piece into a rectangle approximately 12 by 16 inches.

7 Spread the filling evenly over the entire rectangle. Fold in half.

8 Cut alternating triangles every 2 to 3 inches.

9 Starting at the wider end of the triangle, roll up. Place, point side down, on the prepared baking sheet. Repeat to fill and form the other piece of dough.

10 Allow to rise for another 45 to 60 minutes.

11 **Make the syrup:** Combine the sugar and water in a small saucepan and bring to a boil. Lower the heat to medium and cook until the sugar is completely dissolved. Remove from the heat and set aside.

12 Preheat the oven to 350°F.

Note: **Each filling recipe makes enough for an entire batch of dough. You can cut each filling amount in half to make half cinnamon and half chocolate.**

13 Bake the rugelach for 20 to 25 minutes, until just golden brown on top.

14 As soon as the rugelach come out of the oven, brush the sugar syrup all over the pastry. Don't worry about going too crazy; the rugelach will absorb the sugar syrup.

recipe continues

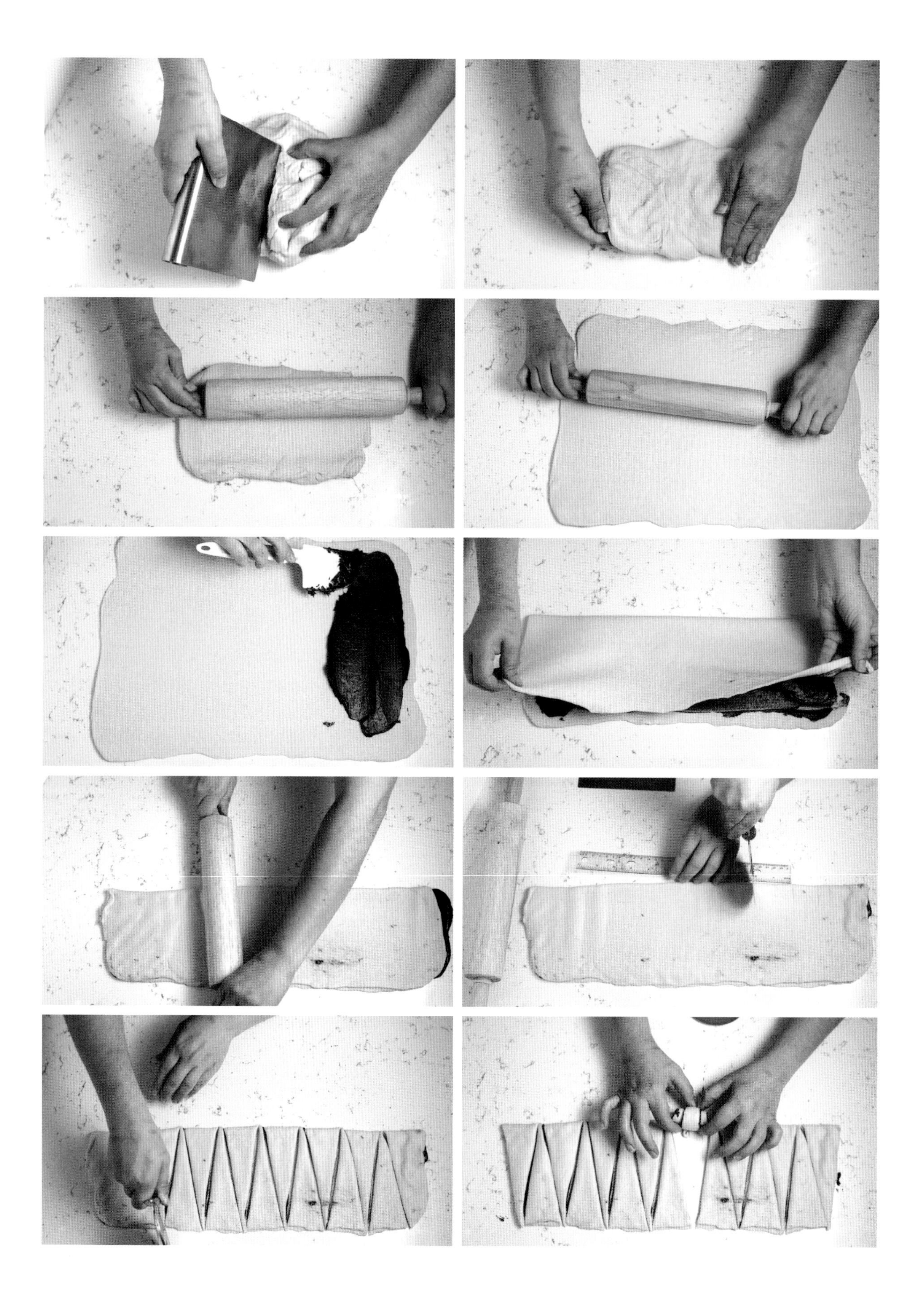

Toffee & Chocolate Mandel Bread

Makes 2 dozen cookies

If you've got a sweet tooth, you will love the sweet, caramelized toffee and chocolate crunch of this mandel bread version. You could also replace the toffee with finely chopped-up leftover Halloween candy.

3 cups unbleached all-purpose flour
2 teaspoons baking powder
½ teaspoon fine sea salt
¾ cup granulated sugar
¼ cup light brown sugar
16 tablespoons (2 sticks) unsalted butter, melted, or 1 cup vegetable, safflower, or canola oil
3 large eggs
1 teaspoon vanilla extract
½ teaspoon almond extract (optional)
1 cup toffee bits
1 cup chopped dark chocolate chips or pieces

1 Combine the flour, baking powder, and salt in a bowl.

2 In a stand mixer fitted with the paddle attachment, beat the melted butter and sugars together until creamy and smooth. Add the eggs, vanilla, and almond extract (if using). Add the flour mixture to the butter mixture in batches and mix until combined.

3 Fold in the chocolate chips and toffee. Form the dough into a disk and wrap in plastic wrap. Place in the fridge for at least 1 to 2 hours, until chilled and firm.

4 When ready to bake, preheat the oven to 350°F and line two baking sheets with parchment paper or silicone baking mats.

5 Split the dough into two equal parts and, on the prepared baking sheets, form each into a log about 2 inches wide, 13 inches long, and 1 inch tall.

6 Bake for 25 minutes, or until golden. Remove from the oven and allow to cool on the pans.

7 Lower the oven temperature to 250°F.

8 When the logs have cooled, using a sharp, serrated knife, cut on the diagonal into pieces around ¾ inch thick.

9 Place each slice back on baking sheets. Bake until they achieve your desired crispness, 35 to 40 minutes.

10 Remove from the oven and allow to cool before serving.

Chocolate & Nut Mandel Bread

Makes 2 dozen cookies

What's the difference between mandel bread and biscotti? Marcy Goldman writes in her classic book *A Treasury of Jewish Holiday Baking* that it's whether a Nonna or a Bubbe is serving them. Italian foods have influenced Jewish foods in many instances, and the same for Jewish foods on Italian cuisine, so it's no surprise that the two are so similar. Biscotti are more commonly made with butter, rather than oil; whereas, because of Jewish dietary laws, you're more likely to find mandel bread made without dairy so that it can be eaten after a meat meal by those observing the kosher laws.

This recipe can be made with butter, oil, or nondairy margarine. I like using mini chocolate chips or chopped-up chocolate for a more even distribution, but use whatever chocolate you prefer or have on hand.

3 cups unbleached all-purpose flour
2 teaspoons baking powder
½ teaspoon fine sea salt
¾ cup granulated sugar
¼ cup light brown sugar
16 tablespoons (2 sticks) unsalted butter, melted, or vegetable, safflower, or canola oil
3 large eggs
1 teaspoon vanilla extract
½ teaspoon almond extract (optional)
1 cup chopped milk or dark chocolate
1 cup chopped walnuts or almonds

1 Combine the flour, baking powder, and salt in a large bowl.

2 In a stand mixer fitted with the paddle attachment, beat the melted butter and sugars together until creamy and smooth. Add the eggs, vanilla, and almond extract (if using). Add the flour mixture to the butter mixture in batches and mix until combined.

3 Fold in the chocolate chips and nuts. Form the dough into a disk and wrap in plastic wrap. Place in the fridge for at least 1 to 2 hours, until chilled and firm.

4 When ready to bake, preheat the oven to 350°F and line two baking sheets with parchment paper or silicone baking mats.

5 Split the dough into two equal parts and, on the prepared baking sheets, form each into a log about 2 inches wide, 13 inches long, and 1 inch tall.

6 Bake for 25 minutes, or until golden. Remove from the oven and allow to cool on the pans.

7 Lower the oven temperature to 250°F.

8 When the logs have cooled, using a sharp, serrated knife, cut them on the diagonal into pieces around ¾ inch thick.

9 Place each slice back on the baking sheets. Bake until they achieve your desired crispness, 35 to 40 minutes.

10 Remove from the oven and allow to cool before serving.

Funfetti Mandel Bread

Makes 2 dozen cookies

Mandel bread have a reputation for being a bit old school, maybe boring, maybe even dry. But these colorful, sweet mandel bread stray far from this stereotype. Top mandel bread with drizzled white chocolate and colored sprinkles for an extra-fun and bright presentation.

For the dough:

3 cups unbleached all-purpose flour

2 teaspoons baking powder

½ teaspoon fine sea salt

¾ cup granulated sugar

¼ cup light brown sugar

16 tablespoons (2 sticks) unsalted butter, melted, or 1 cup vegetable, safflower, or canola oil

3 large eggs

1 teaspoon vanilla extract

½ teaspoon almond extract (optional)

1 cup multicolored sprinkles, plus more for garnish (optional)

½ cup white chocolate chips

½ cup rainbow chips

For the white chocolate drizzle:

1 cup good-quality white chocolate chips or bar broken into pieces

1 tablespoon vegetable or coconut oil

1 **Make the dough:** Combine the flour, baking powder, and salt in a bowl.

2 In a stand mixer fitted with the paddle attachment, beat the melted butter and sugars together until creamy and smooth. Add the eggs, vanilla, and almond extract (if using). Add the flour mixture to the butter mixture in batches and mix until combined.

3 Fold in the sprinkles, white chocolate chips, and rainbow chips. Form the dough into a disk and wrap in plastic wrap. Place in the fridge for at least 1 to 2 hours, until chilled and firm.

4 When ready to bake, preheat the oven to 350°F and line two baking sheets with parchment paper or silicone baking mats.

5 Split the dough into two equal parts and, on the prepared baking sheets, form each into a log about 2 inches wide, 13 inches long, and 1 inch tall.

6 Bake for 25 minutes, or until golden. Remove from the oven and allow to cool on the pans.

7 Lower the oven temperature to 250°F.

8 When the logs have cooled, using a sharp, serrated knife, cut on the diagonal into pieces around ¾ inch thick.

9 Place each slice back on the baking sheets. Bake until they achieve your desired crispness, 35 to 40 minutes.

10 Remove from the oven and allow to cool.

11 **Make the drizzle:** Place the white chocolate and oil in a small, microwave-safe bowl. Microwave at 30-second intervals, stirring in between until completely melted.

12 Drizzle the cookies with the white chocolate and top with additional sprinkles, if desired.

Matzah Toffee

Serves 10 to 12

For so many American Jewish families, it just isn't Passover without matzah toffee. Almost every family I know makes some. That's in part because it's delicious, and in part because it's a fairly easy dessert recipe. Of course, I love having fun with this sweet, adding sprinkles, dried fruit, nuts, and even coconut for exciting variations.

4 matzah sheets
16 tablespoons (2 sticks) unsalted butter or margarine
1 cup packed dark brown sugar
1¼ cups semisweet or dark chocolate chips
¼ teaspoon fine sea salt
½ cup good-quality white chocolate chips (optional)
1½ teaspoons vegetable or coconut oil (optional)

Ideas for Matzah Toffee Toppings

- *Colored sprinkles*
- *Chopped pistachios and dried cranberries*
- *Chopped macadamia nuts and dried pineapple or flaked coconut*
- *Flaky Maldon sea salt*
- *Chopped pecans*

1 Preheat the oven to 375°F. Line a baking sheet with parchment paper.

2 Arrange the matzah in one layer on the prepared baking sheet. Break the matzah into smaller pieces so as to fill the pan completely. Set aside.

3 Melt the butter and brown sugar in a medium saucepan over medium heat, stirring constantly. Once this mixture reaches a boil, cook for a few more minutes, until thickened and starting to pull away from the sides of the pan. Remove from the heat.

4 Pour the toffee mixture over the matzah, gently spreading it with a spatula to cover it with an even layer.

5 Put the matzah pan into the oven and lower the heat to 350°F. Bake for 15 minutes, checking every so often to make sure it doesn't burn.

6 After 15 minutes, the toffee mixture will have bubbled up and turned golden brown. Remove from the oven. Sprinkle the matzah immediately with the chocolate chips. Pop back into the oven for 3 minutes, or until the chocolate has melted slightly. Spread with an offset spatula.

7 Before the chocolate has set is the right time to add any toppings (see suggestions at left).

8 **Optional step:** In a microwave-safe bowl, microwave the white chocolate chips and oil for 30-second intervals until smooth and melted, mixing in between. With a fork, drizzle the white chocolate over the matzah. Then, add any additional toppings.

Apple Tahini Crumble

Serves 6 to 8

When the Jewish New Year comes around, it's common to find apple cake or honey cake on many Ashkenazi tables, since both honey and apple are common ingredients for Rosh Hashanah dishes. But neither of these desserts really excites me. Fruit crumbles are my go-to dessert all year long for a few reasons: They are easy, they come together quickly, and I almost always have some overripe fruit sitting in my fridge or freezer that will be perfect transformed into this comforting dessert.

Apples are a traditional ingredient enjoyed for the Jewish New Year by eastern European Jews. But since the Jewish New Year can often occur at the end of summer, this could be made with peaches, plums, berries, or any combination of fruit that you love. Tahini and Yemenite hawaij coffee spice blend will add a little extra something special if you are inclined. You can also make your own.

Cooking spray for baking dish

For the fruit layer:

7 or 8 medium apples, peeled, cored, and chopped into approximately 1-inch pieces (around 6 cups of chopped apples)
⅓ cup granulated sugar
1 tablespoon cornstarch
1 teaspoon ground cinnamon, pumpkin pie spice, or Hawaij Coffee Spice Blend (recipe follows)
Juice of ½ lemon

For the crumble topping:

1¼ cups unbleached all-purpose flour
⅓ cup packed light brown sugar
¼ cup granulated sugar
¼ teaspoon salt
½ teaspoon ground cinnamon
⅓ cup old-fashioned rolled oats
6 tablespoons unsalted butter, melted
¼ cup tahini

For serving (optional):

Vanilla ice cream or fresh whipped cream
Crumbled halva pieces

1 Preheat the oven to 350°F. Grease a 9-by-11-inch baking dish with cooking spray.

2 **Make the fruit layer:** Combine the apples, granulated sugar, cornstarch, cinnamon, and lemon juice in a large bowl.

3 **Make the crumble:** In a separate bowl, combine all the crumble ingredients, using a wooden spoon, until evenly mixed but there are still clumps.

4 Pour the apple mixture in an even layer into the prepared baking dish.

5 Sprinkle the crumble topping evenly on top of the apples until they are almost entirely covered.

6 Bake, uncovered, for 45 to 60 minutes, until the apple mixture is bubbling and the crumble is golden brown. If the crumbs seem to be getting too dark, you can cover the dish with foil.

7 Serve warm or at room temperature with vanilla ice cream or fresh whipped cream and an extra sprinkle of halva, if desired.

recipe continues

Hawaij Coffee Spice Blend

Makes ¼ cup

Hawaij is a Yemenite spice blend that has become popular throughout Israel. There are actually two versions of hawaij, one for soup that is more savory (see page 22), and this one intended for your coffee. It is also fantastic for baking projects. Try some in your cookies, mandel bread, coffee cake, babka, and the Apple Tahini Crumble (page 191).

1 teaspoon ground cinnamon
1 teaspoon ground cardamom
1 teaspoon ground ginger
1 teaspoon freshly grated nutmeg
1 teaspoon ground cloves

1 Combine all the ingredients in a small bowl.

2 Store in an airtight container.

Passover Fruit Crumble

Serves 6 to 8

Although this is definitely a dessert, I have been known to make this dish and serve it with some Greek yogurt as a breakfast during Passover. If you want to make this gluten-free, you could use all almond flour or another gluten-free flour for the topping.

Cooking spray for baking dish

For the fruit layer:

6 to 8 cups fresh or frozen fruit, such as berries, peaches, apples, or a combination

⅓ cup granulated sugar

1 tablespoon cornstarch or potato starch (optional)

1 teaspoon ground cinnamon

Juice of ½ lemon

For the crumble topping:

½ cup almond flour

½ cup matzah cake meal

¼ teaspoon sea salt

⅔ cup packed light brown sugar

1 cup chopped nuts, such as almonds, walnuts, or a combination

4 tablespoons (½ stick) unsalted butter or margarine, melted

Vanilla ice cream for serving (optional)

1 Preheat the oven to 350°F. Grease a 9-by-11-inch baking dish with cooking spray.

2 **Make the fruit layer:** Combine the fruit, granulated sugar, cornstarch (if using), cinnamon, and lemon juice in a bowl.

3 **Make the crumble topping:** In a separate bowl, combine all the crumble ingredients, using a wooden spoon, until evenly mixed but there are still clumps.

4 Pour the fruit mixture in an even layer into the prepared baking dish.

5 Sprinkle the crumble topping evenly on top of the fruit until it is almost entirely covered.

6 Bake, uncovered, for 45 to 60 minutes, until the fruit mixture is bubbling and the crumble is golden brown. If the crumbs are getting too dark, you can cover the dish with foil.

7 Serve warm or at room temperature with vanilla ice cream, if desired.

Rainbow Cookies

Serves 8 to 10

Three-layer tricolor rainbow cookies are actually not really Jewish in origin, but Italian—the red, white, and green is a nod to the Italian flag. But you would be hard pressed to find a kosher bakery or Jewish *kiddush* spread without some rainbow cookies in the mix. These almond-flavored cakelike cookies were introduced to Jewish immigrants in New York by their Italian neighbors. When done right, they are sheer perfection and one of the most nostalgic foods in my family.

Cooking spray for pans
All-purpose flour for pans

For the cake:

4 large eggs
1 cup sugar
4 ounces almond paste, broken into little pieces or processed in a food processor for 30 seconds
16 tablespoons (2 sticks) unsalted butter, melted
1 cup unbleached all-purpose flour
½ teaspoon salt
½ teaspoon vanilla extract
Red and green food coloring (about 8 drops each)

For the chocolate glaze:

1 cup dark or semisweet chocolate chips
1 tablespoon vegetable shortening or vegetable oil
Pinch of salt

For the filling:

Raspberry or apricot jam

Special equipment:

Three 8-inch square baking pans
Food scale
Offset spatula
Sharp knife

1 Preheat the oven to 350°F. Grease three 8-inch square baking pans with cooking spray. Line the bottom of each pan with parchment paper, grease again, and add a light dusting of flour. Tap each pan to remove any excess flour.

2 **Make the cake:** Using a handheld mixer and large bowl or a stand mixer fitted with the whisk attachment, mix the eggs and sugar until thick and yellow. Add the crumbled almond paste and combine.

3 Mix in the melted butter, flour, salt, and vanilla.

4 Weigh the batter using a food scale and then divide it into three equal amounts. Add green food coloring to one batch of batter. Add red food coloring to a second batch of batter. Leave the third batch without any additional food coloring (this is your white layer).

5 Pour a single batch of batter into a prepared pan. Repeat with the other two batches and prepared pans. Bake for 8 to 9 minutes, until just set and no longer wet in the middle.

6 Remove from the oven and allow to cool completely on a wire rack.

7 **Make the glaze:** Place the chocolate, shortening, and salt in a microwave-safe bowl. Microwave for 30-second intervals until melted. Stir vigorously to ensure there are no clumps.

8 Place a piece of parchment paper on top of a platter or baking sheet. Place the red cake layer on the parchment paper. Spread with a thin layer of raspberry jam. Top with the white cake layer. Add another thin layer of raspberry jam. Top with the green cake layer.

9 Carefully spread half of the chocolate glaze on top. Place in the refrigerator to chill for 15 to 20 minutes, until completely hard.

10 Turn the entire cake over and spread the remaining chocolate glaze on the other side. Place back in the refrigerator to chill for 30 minutes or overnight.

11 Use a sharp knife to trim the edges and slice the cake into cookies.

Passover Rainbow Cookies

Serves 8 to 10

These Passover-friendly rainbow cookies are so good, no one will ever know they are different from the kind you would serve all year. They can be made ahead of time and store well for several days in an airtight container.

Cooking spray for pans

All-purpose flour for pans

For the cake:

4 large eggs

1 cup sugar

4 ounces almond paste, broken into little pieces or processed in a food processor for 30 seconds

16 tablespoons (2 sticks) unsalted butter, melted

½ cup almond flour

½ cup matzah cake meal

½ teaspoon salt

½ teaspoon vanilla extract

Red and green food coloring (about 8 drops each)

For the chocolate glaze:

1 cup dark or semisweet chocolate chips

1 tablespoon vegetable shortening or vegetable oil

Pinch of salt

For the filling:

Raspberry or apricot jam

Special equipment:

Three 8-inch square baking pans

Food scale

Offset spatula

Sharp knife

1 Preheat the oven to 350°F. Grease three 8-inch square baking pans with cooking spray. Line the bottom of each pan with parchment paper, grease again, and add a light dusting of flour. Tap each pan to remove any excess flour.

2 **Make the cake:** Using a handheld mixer and a large bowl or a stand mixer fitted with the whisk attachment, mix the eggs and sugar until thick and yellow. Add the crumbled almond paste and combine.

3 Mix in the melted butter, flour, salt, and vanilla.

4 Weigh the batter, using a food scale, and then divide it into three equal amounts. Add green food coloring to one batch of batter. Add red food coloring to a second batch of batter. Leave the third batch without any additional food coloring (this is your white layer).

5 Pour a single batch of batter into each prepared pan. Repeat with the other two batches and prepared pans. Bake for 8 to 9 minutes, until just set and no longer wet in the middle.

6 Remove from the oven and allow to cool completely on a wire rack.

7 **Make the glaze:** Place the chocolate, shortening, and salt in a microwave-safe bowl. Microwave for 30-second intervals until melted. Stir vigorously to ensure there are no clumps.

8 Place a piece of parchment paper on top of a platter or baking sheet. Place the red cake layer on the parchment paper. Spread with thin layer of raspberry jam. Top with the white cake layer. Add another thin layer of raspberry jam. Top with the green cake layer.

9 Carefully spread half of the chocolate glaze on top. Place in the refrigerator to chill for 15 to 20 minutes, until completely hard.

10 Turn over and spread the remaining chocolate glaze on the other side. Place back in the refrigerator to chill for 30 minutes or overnight.

11 Use a sharp knife to trim the edges and slice the cake into cookies.

Basic New York–Style Cheesecake

Serves 6 to 8

This is your simple, creamy, basic, and absolutely delicious cheesecake. Serve with fresh berries and whipped cream, and dig in.

Cooking spray for pan

For the crust:

1½ cups cookie crumbs

6 tablespoons unsalted butter, melted

¼ teaspoon salt

1 tablespoon sugar

For the filling:

Three 8-ounce packages full-fat cream cheese, at room temperature

1 cup sugar

2 teaspoons vanilla extract

1 cup full-fat sour cream

4 large eggs

Special equipment:

8- or 9-inch springform pan

1 Preheat the oven to 375°F. Grease an 8- or 9-inch springform pan with cooking spray and line with parchment paper.

2 **Make the crust:** Combine the cookie crumbs, melted butter, salt, and sugar in a bowl.

3 Press the cookie mixture in an even layer into the bottom of the prepared pan and slightly up the sides. Using a measuring cup can help evenly press the mixture into the bottom and sides.

4 Bake the crust for 10 minutes. Remove from the oven and allow to cool.

5 Lower the oven temperature to 325°F.

6 **Make the filling:** Using a stand mixer fitted with the paddle attachment or a handheld mixer and a large bowl, beat the cream cheese and sugar until smooth, 2 to 3 minutes. Add the vanilla and sour cream and mix again for 1 minute.

7 Add the eggs, one at a time, and mix until incorporated. Pour the mixture into the prepared crust.

8 Cover the bottom of the springform pan with foil. Boil water in a teakettle or pot.

9 Place the springform pan in a larger baking dish. Place in the oven and pour enough boiling water into the baking dish to reach halfway up the outside of the springform pan.

10 Bake for 1 hour.

11 After 1 hour, turn off the oven and crack open the door (you can stick a wooden spoon in the door to keep it open). After 1 hour of cooling in the oven, remove from the oven and the baking dish, and allow to chill in its springform pan in the fridge for 6 to 8 hours, or overnight.

Cookie Butter Cheesecake

Serves 6 to 8

If you're not familiar with cookie butter (also known as speculoos), prepare to fall in love. Made from European speculoos cookies, it is creamy and rich. It is available kosher, but you will have to buy it at a kosher market. Trader Joe's sells its own version and most major supermarkets will carry it in the peanut butter and jam section.

Cooking spray for pan

For the crust:

1½ cups speculoos cookie crumbs

6 tablespoons unsalted butter, melted

¼ teaspoon salt

1 tablespoon sugar

For the filling:

Three 8-ounce packages full-fat cream cheese, at room temperature

1 cup sugar

2 teaspoons vanilla extract

1 cup full-fat sour cream

4 large eggs

⅓ cup cookie butter

Special equipment:

8- to 9-inch springform pan

1 Preheat the oven to 375°F. Grease an 8- or 9-inch springform pan and line with parchment paper.

2 **Make the crust:** Combine the cookie crumbs, melted butter, salt, and sugar in a medium bowl.

3 Press the cookie mixture in an even layer into the bottom of the prepared pan and slightly up the sides. Using a measuring cup can help evenly press the mixture into the bottom and sides.

4 Bake the crust for 10 minutes. Remove from the oven and allow to cool.

5 Lower the oven temperature to 325°F.

6 Using a stand mixer fitted with the paddele attachment or a handheld mixer and a large bowl, beat the cream cheese until smooth, 2 to 3 minutes. Add the vanilla and sour cream and mix again for 1 minute.

7 Add the eggs, one at a time, and mix until incorporated. Remove ½ cup of the filling, place in a small bowl, and mix the cookie butter into it.

8 Pour the rest of the cream cheese filling into the crust. Top with the cookie butter filling and swirl together.

9 Cover the bottom of the springform pan with foil. Boil water in a teakettle or pot.

10 Place the springform pan in a larger baking dish. Place in the oven and pour enough boiling water into the baking dish to reach halfway up the outside of the springform pan.

11 Bake for 1 hour.

12 After 1 hour, turn off the oven and crack open the door (you can stick a wooden spoon in the door to keep it open). After 1 hour of cooling in the oven, remove from the oven and the baking dish, and allow to chill in its springform pan in the fridge for 6 to 8 hours, or overnight.

Cheesecake

Cheesecake might seem as American as, say, apple pie. But like many other foods that are synonymous with New York, it was introduced to Americans by none other than eastern European Jewish immigrants. Cheesecake is a traditional food that is enjoyed for Shavuot, a holiday when it is customary to eat dairy-heavy foods. But, to me, cheesecake is an all-year sweet to enjoy for celebratory occasions. And it's also a great Passover-friendly dessert.

However, here is my disclaimer: you cannot cut corners when making cheesecake. There are no-bake cheesecake recipes, and those truly are wonderful. But if you are going to bake a cheesecake, there are several steps you must follow for creamy, no-crack cheesecake:

1. Use full-fat dairy products. Period. Save the nonfat yogurt for breakfast and smoothies.
2. You must bake it in a bain-marie (a water bath). This will ensure even, slow baking all the way around.
3. Bake it at a low temperature, and then allow it to cool slowly by cracking open the oven.
4. Allow the cheesecake to cool completely before serving. This means you will need to plan ahead.

Gluten-Free Mango Cheesecake

with Coconut Almond Crust

Serves 6 to 8

Cheesecake is a great dessert for a gluten-free diet or for during Passover. Of course, you can make cheesecake without any crust, but I still enjoy the contrast between creamy filling and a little sweet, nutty, crunchy bite at the bottom.

Cooking spray for pan

For the crust:

1 cup sweetened shredded coconut

1¼ cups sliced almonds

6 tablespoons unsalted butter, melted

¼ teaspoon salt

2 tablespoons coconut flour, almond flour, or matzah cake meal

For the filling:

Three 8-ounce packages full-fat cream cheese, at room temperature

1 cup sugar

2 teaspoons vanilla extract

1 cup full-fat sour cream

4 large eggs

¾ cup fresh or frozen mango, pureed

Special equipment:

8- to 9-inch springform pan

1 Preheat the oven to 375°F. Grease an 8- or 9-inch springform pan with cooking spray and line with parchment paper.

2 **Make the crust:** Combine the cookie crumbs, melted butter, salt, and sugar in a medium bowl.

3 Press the cookie mixture in an even layer into the bottom of the pan and slightly up the sides. Using a measuring cup can help evenly press the mixture into the bottom and sides.

4 Bake for 10 minutes. Remove from the oven and let cool. Lower the oven temperature to 325°F.

5 **Make the filling:** Using a stand mixer fitted with the paddle attachment or a handheld mixer and a large bowl, beat the cream cheese until smooth, 2 to 3 minutes. Add the vanilla and sour cream and mix again for 1 minute.

6 Add the eggs, one at a time, and mix until incorporated. Remove 1 cup of the cream cheese filling, place in a small bowl, and mix the mango puree unto it.

7 Pour the rest of the cream cheese mixture into the prepared crust. Top with the mango filling mixture and swirl.

8 Cover the bottom of the springform pan with foil. Boil water in a teakettle or pot.

9 Place the springform pan into a larger baking dish. Place in the oven and pour enough boiling water into the baking dish to reach halfway up the outside of the springform pan.

10 Bake for 1 hour. After 1 hour, turn off the oven and crack open the door (you can stick a wooden spoon in the door to keep it open). After 1 hour of cooling in the oven, remove from the baking dish and chill in the pan in the fridge for 6 to 8 hours, or overnight.

Acknowledgments

Thank you to my wonderful agent, Judy Linden, for helping this project finally come to fruition. So many thank-yous to Ann Treistman at Countryman Press, for supporting a young working mom in all the ways. Many thanks to art director, Allison Chi, for your patience and hard work.

My endless love and thanks to my partner in all things, my husband, Jonathan, for all his support, creativity, fat kid energy, and willingness to taste everything and to always give honest feedback. Also thank you for helping keep the kids alive.

I want to thank all my coworkers at 70 Faces Media, especially Deborah Kolben, Molly Tolsky, Lisa Keys, Shevy Baskin, Becky Phillips, and Rachel Myerson, for working together all these years, teaching me, laughing together, and generally putting up with me day in, day out.

Thank you to my friend Danielle Feinberg, for being my thought partner in organizing the concept for this book, recipe testing, driving me nuts with your icing precision, and supporting me in all the ways a wonderful friend does.

A very special thank you to Miriam Golan and Sylvia Fallas, for their willingness to answer all my questions and for sharing their overwhelming Syrian warmth, generosity, and expert food knowledge.

Thank you to my colleagues and friends, Susan Barocas and Leah Koenig, for sharing your time and expertise with me.

Thank you to Sarah and Yuval Brokman, for sharing so many beloved family recipes for this project, and always being willing to make an extra kugel.

Thank you to Gina Vinick, for spending such a beautiful afternoon together, and for teaching me to make your mom's kugel. Your mom's recipe will continue to live on. Thanks to Merisa, for sharing your mom with me.

My sister-in-law Becca helped make my first book come alive, and she never stops pushing me to do my best. Thank you to a person who is more than family, more than a friend, more than a colleague.

To Sheri Silver and Doug Schneider—there are not enough thank-yous or words to give due respect to our friendship and partnership all these years. What a blessing it has been to know you, working together and creating delicious things.

Thank you to my dear friend and colleague of many years, Sonya Sanford, for being a sounding board and thought partner, and for dropping everything to take some photos.

To Poppy, Jojo, Grandy, Roro, Uncle Baba, Aunt Kappy, Uncle Jon, Uncle Danny, and Uncle Ninan—thank you for your love and support. I am so lucky to have family like you to eat my food, cheer me on, and love me.

To my Illumiyentas—your wit, humor, and brilliance give me life, make me think, and lift me up. Thank you for your support and friendship.

Thank you to my troop of volunteer recipe testers, including Jessica Fox, Jana Kadden, Kimberly Tower, Elissa and Daniel Kestin, Lisa Buber, and Jennifer Stempel. Your generosity and time ensures these recipes actually work!

To my friends and colleagues Jacqueline Hensel, Danielle Sarna Praport, and Rachel Ringler, for their never-ending support and love.

A special thank-you to my favorite butcher and a true mensch, Harold Roy, for always making sure I am stocked with the best-quality meat.

The biggest carb-loving thank-you to Aliza Plotkin and the entire Modern Jewish Baker Facebook group for bringing such positivity and support into my life, and for giving me the confidence to do this crazy book writing thing again. Thank you to my Instagram followers for sharing this journey together and for cheering me on. Social media is so much more than marketing to me, and I am grateful to have found community and friends in you.

To my children, you are my everything.

Index

Page numbers in *italics* indicate photos.

Q

R

S

About the Author

SHANNON SARNA is founding editor of *The Nosher*, the widest-reaching website dedicated to Jewish food, which is part of the 70 Faces Media group. Shannon grew up in upstate New York immersed in performance and music as well as surrounded by diverse culinary experiences: Her Sicilian American mother loved to bake, her Ashkenazi Jewish father loved to experiment, and her grandfather was a food chemist who patented Tang, among other products. Her writing and recipes have been featured in *Bake from Scratch Magazine*, *Taste of Home Magazine*, *Parade Magazine*, Food52, The Kitchn, *Tablet Magazine*, JTA News, *New Jersey Monthly Magazine*, Vinepair, and Modern Loss. She graduated from Smith College in Northampton, Massachusetts, with a degree in comparative government and Spanish language and literature and lives in South Orange, New Jersey, with her husband, three children, two rescue dogs, and a bunny named S'mores. Her first cookbook, *Modern Jewish Baker: Challah, Babka, Bagels & More*, was released in September 2017 by Countryman Press.